BUSINESS CARD

ROCKPORT
PUBLISHERS

ROCKPORT PUBLISHERS, INC.
ROCKPORT, MASSACHUSETTS

First published in the United States of America by:
Rockport Publishers, Inc.
146 Granite Street
Rockport, Massachusetts 01966-1299
Telephone: (508) 546-9590
Fax: (508) 546-7141

ISBN 1-56496-292-X

10 9 8 7 6 5 4 3 2 1

Layout: Sara Day Graphic Design
Cover credits: Blue Sky Design, Blink, 13th Floor, Greteman Group,
    Robin Lipner Digital, Joan C. Hollingsworth, Barbara Raab Design, Design
    Center, Michael Courtney Design, Hornall Anderson Design Works, Glazer
    Graphics, Edmunds Jones Design, Two In Design, Phoenix Creative.

Manufactured in Singapore by Welpac

Introduction

It's amazing how, in this era of the Internet, e-mail, faxes and cellular communications, that the business card remains the best reminder of a professional encounter. The power one draws upon in his field lays not in the millions of bits a desktop computer can process per second, or how "wired" he is to cyberspace, or even how many people can be influenced by a broadcast fax. Instead, the benchmark is still "how rarified are the cards in your Rolodex?"

Business cards show class. Business cards show style. Business cards are a snapshot that recalls an impression in the memory long after the encounter is over. Some cards can make people look more "rarified," propelling them beyond the executive gatekeepers who prevent the competition from getting through.

In Design Library: Business Cards, the best business cards in circulation have found their way here, the favorites Rockport has adjudicated in its many design contests. The brightest designers, representing many countries, are published in this book, showing readers how they themselves can use the business card to open doors to better business communication.

❶
Design Firm
Antero Ferreira Design
Art Director
Antero Ferreira
Designer
Antero Ferreira, Eduardo
Sotto Mayor
Illustrator
Eduardo Sotto Mayor
Client
Padaria Cristal

❷
Design Firm
Tangram Strategic Design
Art Director
Enrico Sempi
Designer
Enrico Sempi
Client
Eliana Lorena

❸
Design Firm
Michael Stanard Inc.
Art Director
Michael Stanard
Design
Lisa Fingerhut
Client
Caledonian Incorporated

❹
Design Firm
Peter Hollingsworth &
Associates
Designer
Steven John Wammack
Client
Ray Troxell Associates
Architects

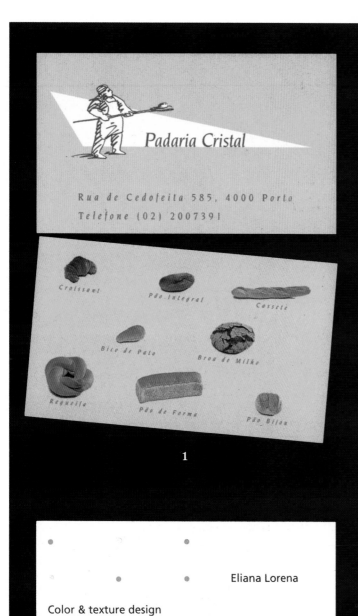

1

3

2

4

1

ATHENA CREATIVE GROUP

BARBARA RAAB

3105 VALLEY DRIVE

ALEXANDRIA, VIRGINIA

22302

671 1329

2

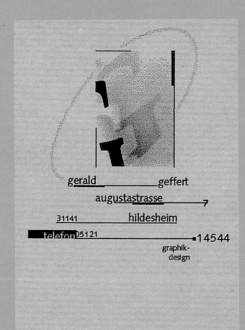

gerald   geffert
augustastrasse   7
31141   hildesheim
telefon 05121   14544
graphik-
design

ATHENA
creative

3

Robert Beckon
photography

pager 612-661-4480
612.874.1218

4

Karin Nødskov-Holm

KNOWLEDGE TRANSFER
Postbox 94 • 2970 Hørsholm
45 76 00 75 • Fax 45 66 43 14

1

2

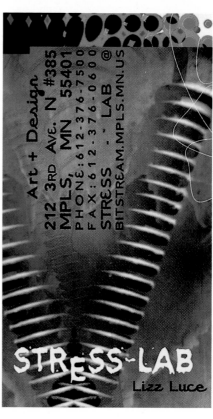

1 Design Firm
Jacqué Consulting Inc.
Designer
Crystal Folgman
Client
Self-promotion
Graphic design

2 Design Firm
Stress Lab
Designer
J.C. Munson
Client
Self-promotion
Graphic design

❶
Design Firm
Graphic Partners
Designer
Mark Ross
Client
Orr Macqueen W.S.
Corporate & Commercial
Solicitors

❷
Design Firm
Loma Stovall Design
Art Director
Loma Stovall
Designer
Loma Stovall
Client
Printology

❸
Design Firm
Champ/Cotter
Designer
Heather Champ
Client
Suzan Piovaty Designer

❹
Design Firm
Planet Design Co.
Art Director
Planet Design Co.
Designer
Planet Design Co.
Client
Lindsay, Stone & Briggs
Advertising Inc.

❺
Design Firm
Jeff Labbe Illustrator
Designer
Jeff Labbe
Client
Jeff Labbe

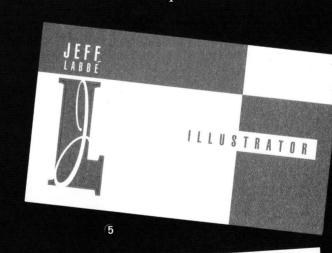

ORR MACQUEEN W.S.
CORPORATE & COMMERCIAL SOLICITORS

JONATHAN R.M. MacQUEEN   36 Heriot Row
Partner   Edinburgh EH3 6ES
Tel: 031 225 3366
Fax: 031 225 2210

①

ADVERTISING
LINDSAY, STONE & BRIGGS
INCORPORATED

ART DIRECTOR
100 STATE STREET, MADISON, WI 53703
PHONE (608) 251 7070 FAX (608) 251 8989

④

PRINTOLOGY

Stefano Introini

The Science of Impression
1291 Electric Avenue, Venice, CA 90291

310.392.1878 Fax: 310.399.5151

2

JEFF
LABBÉ
ILLUSTRATOR

⑤

SUZAN PIOVATY

DESIGNER

③

218 PRINCETON AVE. CLAREMONT, CA. 91711
FŌN 909-621-6678

1 Design Firm
Recla Business Services
Designer
Claudia Werner
Client
Self-promotion
Business marketing services

2 Design Firm
ImageWright, Inc.
Designer
Jeffrey L. Belk
Client
Self-promotion
Design

3 Design Firm
Greteman Group
Designer
Sonia Greteman
Client
Pechin Construction

4 Design Firm
Greteman Group
Designers
Sonia Greteman, Bill Gardner
Client
Equity Standard
Numismatics rare coin brokerage

1

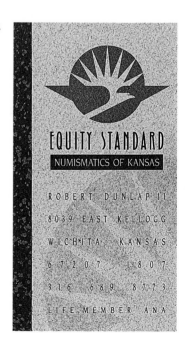

2

3

4

STEVEN COOK

FREELANCE ANESTHESIA SERVICES
4300 WEST FRANCISCO DRIVE, #28
PENSACOLA, FLORIDA 32504
(904) 433-6063
1-800-946-4646 PIN 1168064

1 Design Firm
Arminda Hopkins
and Associates
Designer
Melanie Matson
Client
Steven Cook
Freelance anesthesia services

2 Design Firm
FORMA LTD.
Designer
Allen Porter
Client
Self-promotion
Design

3 Design Firm
Holden & Company
Designer
Cathe Holden
Photographer
Alan Campbell
Client
Linkages
Mailing services

FORMA

Forma Ltd.
903 Forest Avenue
Evanston, Illinois 60202
Tel 708.328.6145
Fax 708.328.5110

Design/Planning
Marketing Communications

ALLEN PORTER *President*

LINKAGES

PATRICK TEMPLE

LINKAGES MAILING SERVICE
3200 DUTTON AVENUE #222
SANTA ROSA, CA 95407-5733
707-573-9878   FAX 573-1043

❶

Design Firm
Wallace Church
Associates Inc.
Art Director
Stanley Church
Designers
Stanley Church,
Joe Cuticone
Illustrator
Joe Cuticone
Client
Shaw Nautical

❷

Design Firm
Rochelle Seltzer Design
Art Director
Rochelle Seltzer
Designer
Rochelle Seltzer
Client
Rochelle Seltzer

❸

Design Firm
Glenn Martinez &
Associates
Art Director
Kathleen Nelson
Designer
Glenn Martinez
Client
Just Your Type
Service Bureau

❹

Design Firm
Westwood & Associates
Art Director
David Westwood
Designer
David Westwood
Client
Westwood & Associates

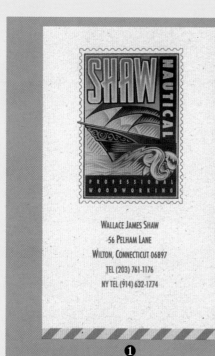

❶

❸

❷

❹

1

SAGE BRUSH DESIGN

DANIELLE BEWER

403 West Channel Road
Santa Monica, California 90402
Tel. 310·459·7487 Fax 310·459·5508

2

Art Company London

Michael J. Goodson
PRESIDENT

Eleven East Wisconsin
Suite 200
Trenton, Illinois 62293
618 224-9435
FAX:
618 224-9296

3

8935 Manchester
Saint Louis
Missouri 63144

Telephone: 961-1985
Area Code 314

1 Design Firm
Sage Brush Design
Designer
Danielle Bewer
Client
Self-promotion
Art and graphic design

2 Design Firm
Phoenix Creative
Designer
Ed Mantels-Seeker
Client
Art Company London
Antique painting reproduction and wholesale

3 Design Firm
Phoenix Creative
Designer
Ed Mantels-Seeker
Client
The Gifted Gardener
Gardening gifts, accessories, and furniture retail

Bras Bike Brand

Design Firm
Animus Comunicaçáo
Designer
Felício Torres
Art Director
Rique Nitzsche

This simple logo can be easily reproduced
at low-cost on T-shirts and direct mailings.

1

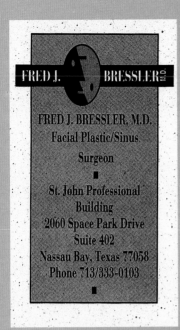

FRED J. BRESSLER, M.D.
Facial Plastic/Sinus
Surgeon

St. John Professional
Building
2060 Space Park Drive
Suite 402
Nassau Bay, Texas 77058
Phone 713/333-0103

3

2

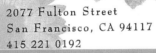

FRANK WIEDEMANN

2077 Fulton Street
San Francisco, CA 94117
415 221 0192

1 Design Firm
MAH Design Inc.
Designer
Mary Anne Heckman
Illustrator
Mary Anne Heckman, Jack Slattery
Client
Fred J. Bressler, M.D.
Facial and plastic surgery

2 Design Firm
Wiedemann Design
Designer
Frank Wiedemann
Photographer
Frank Wiedemann
Client
Self-promotion
Graphic design

3 Design Firm
Zubi Design
Designer
Kristen Balouch
Client
Self-promotion
Design

4 Design Firm
Peterson & Company
Art Director
Bryan L. Peterson
Designer
Bryan L. Peterson
Illustrator
Jan Wilson
Client
John Wong Photography

5 Design Firm
Stress Lab
Designer
Lizz Luce
Client
Cindy Klabechek
Hair and makeup stylist

4

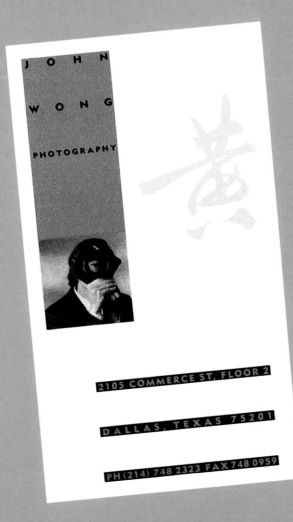

5

1

LA BOULANGERIE

FRENCH BAKERY & CAFE

730 West Shaw Ave.

Fig Garden Village

Fresno, CA 93704

209-222-0555

FAX 209-222-9632

2

Wade Koniakowsky, V.P. Creative Director

dGWB
Advertising

20 Executive Park, Suite 200
Irvine, California 92714
714-863-0404 Fax 714-863-0933

3

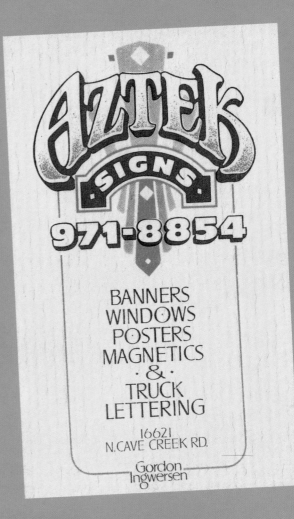

AZTEK SIGNS
971-8854
BANNERS
WINDOWS
POSTERS
MAGNETICS
· & ·
TRUCK
LETTERING
16621
N.CAVE CREEK RD.
Gordon
Ingwersen

4

tmb
clínica cirúrgica

DR. GILSON BARRETO

cirurgia oncológica
crm 59.280

R. Ferreira de Almeida, 70 - Jdm. Guanabara
Fone: 41-5425 - CEP 13073-380
Campinas - SP

1 Design Firm
Shields Design
Art Director
Charles Shields
Designer
Laura Thornton
Illustrator
Laura Thornton
Client
La Boulangerie
Bakery

2 Design Firm
dGWB Advertising
Designer
Michelle Harbord
Client
Self-promotion
Advertising

3 Design Firm
Aztek Signs
Designer
Gordon Ingwersen
Client
Self-promotion
Sign design

4 Design Firm
Recla Business Services
Designer
Claudia Werner
Client
TMB
Medical branch

1

CAROLINE STRANGE OPTICIANS

CIDNEYVINALL

201 GALISTEO
SANTA FE, NEW MEXICO 87501
505-988-9510
FAX: 505-988-1832

2

CORNUCOPIA
ON · THE · WHARF

Kristine Fayerman-Piatt
General Manager

100 Atlantic Avenue
Boston. MA 02110

617.367.0300 Telephone
617.367.8772 Facsimile

3

Law Offices of
LANCE A. LICHTER

TEL
414 375-6868

FAX
414 375-6869

W62 N551
Washington Avenue Cedarburg, Wisconsin
53012

4

intoto
11718 administration Drive
saint louis, missouri 63146
314.995.9970

tricia
stylist

IN TOTO
A salon for men and women

1 **Design Firm**
Cisneros Design
Designer
Fred Cisneros
Client
Caroline Strange Opticians
Unique eyewear retail and optometry

2 **Design Firm**
Laughlin/Winkler Inc.
Designers
Mark Laughlin, Ellen Winkler
Illustrator
Tom Piatt, Ellen Winkler
Client
Cornucopia
Restaurant

3 **Design Firm**
Becker Design
Designer
Neil Becker
Client
Lance Lichter Law Office

4 **Design Firm**
Phoenix Creative
Designer
Eric Thoelke
Client
In Toto Salon
Hair design studio

❶
Design Firm
ICONS
Art Director
Glenn Scott Johnson
Designer
Glenn Scott Johnson
Illustrator
Glenn Scott Johnson
Client
ICONS

❷
Design Firm
Design Group Cook
Art Director
Ken Cook
Designer
Ken Cook
Client
Pat Edwards Photography

❸
Design Firm
Michael Stanard Inc.
Art Director
Lisa Fingerhut
Designer
Michael Stanard
Client
Denise Stanard

❶

GRAPHIC DESIGN
•
ILLUSTRATION

GLENN S. JOHNSON
76 ELM ST. SUITE 313
BOSTON, MA. 02130
617 · 522 · 0165

❷

DENISE STANARD
HAIR DESIGNER
708-259-9977

❸

1

JOHN OAT

ART DIRECTION
COMPUTER GRAPHICS
DESIGN & ILLUSTRATION

8900 Tarrytown Drive
Richmond, Virginia 23229
Phone/Fax (804) 741-8649

2

Phillip Esparza

photographer

3711 Parry Avenue

Suite 103

Dallas Texas 75226

214.823.9782

214.823.9784 fax

p.e.

3

WESTMINSTER
CHRISTIAN
FELLOWSHIP

REV. HARRY METZGER

16670 Easton Avenue

Prairie View, Illinois 60069

708.367.1034

4

TRACS

Technical
Research
and
Consulting
Service

Ron Kukas

1128 W. Evergreen

Visalia, CA 93277

Phone or Fax:

209-627-6971

Mobile:

209-730-2244

5

ANTIQUES
RUSSELL P. ROUSHON
296 TAUGWONK ROAD
STONINGTON, CT 06378
SHOP 203.535.4483
RESIDENCE 203.535.9170

FREELANCE CAMERAMAN
STEVE BREASHEARS
2822 KINNEY DRIVE
WALNUT CREEK, CA 94595
510/937-2174

1 Design Firm
John Oat Communication Arts
Designer
John Oat
Client
Self-promotion
Graphic design

2 Design Firm
Gibbs Baronet
Art Directors
Steve Gibbs, Willie Baronet
Designers
Kellye Kimball, Steve Gibbs
Illustrator
Kellye Kimball
Client
Phillip Esparza
Photography

3 Design Firm
Associates Design
Designer
Beth Finn
Client
Westminster Christian Fellowship

4 Design Firm
Covi Corporation
Agency Gillham & Associates
Designer
Mona Howell
Illustrator
Mona Howell
Client
Tracs
Soil and pesticide consulting

5 Design Firm
PhD
Designer
Terri Haas
Client
Antiques

6 Design Firm
B3 Design
Designer
Barbara B. Breashears
Client
Steve Breashears
Freelance cameraman

❶
Design Firm
The Leonhardt Group
Art Director
Janet Kruse
Designer
Traci Daberko
Illustrator
Julie Paschkis
Client
Turnipseed Brothers

❷
Design Firm
ICONS
Art Director
Glenn Scott Johnson
Designer
Glenn Scott Johnson
Illustrator
Glenn Scott Johnson
Client
Vicki Lee Boyajian

❸
Design Firm
Frank D'Astolfo Design
Art Director
Frank D'Astolfo
Designer
Frank D'Astolfo
Client
Angelica Kitchen

❹
Design Firm
Ascent Communications
Art Director
Allen Haeger
Designer
Allen Haeger
Client
Hope Springs, Inc.

❶

❷

❸

❹

❶

Design Firm
Eilts Anderson Tracy
Art Direction
Patrice Eilts
Designer
Patrice Eilts
Illustrators
Patrice Eilts, Rich Kobs
Client
PB&J Restaurants
Grand St. Cafe

❷

Design Firm
Watch! Graphic Design
Designer
Bruno Watel
Illustrator
Bruno Watel
Client
Styles Unlimited

❸

Design Firm
Mallen and Friends
Advertising Arts & Design
Art Director
Gary Mallen
Designer
Gary Mallen
Client
Mallen and Friends
Advertising Arts & Design

❹

Design Firm
Mark Palmer Design
Art Director
Mark Palmer
Designer
Mark Palmer
Illustrator
Curtis Palmer
Client
Southwest Landscape

❶

GRAND ST.
CAFE

DANA WOLLERMAN

4740 Grand

Kansas City, Missouri

64112

(816) 561-8000

STYLES
UNLIMITED
PROFESSIONAL HAIRCARE

YOUR NEXT APPOINTMENT IS

WITH:

DAY: DATE   TIME

IF UNABLE TO KEEP APPOINTMENT, PLEASE
GIVE US 24 HOUR NOTICE, THANK-YOU

STYLES
UNLIMITED
PROFESSIONAL HAIRCARE

5335 NORTH CLARK

CHICAGO, IL 60640

(312) 561-5566

2

Mallen
And Friends
Advertising Arts &
Design

Jani   Duncan

8522 Cherokee Lane

Leawood, KS 66206

(913) 341-7300

FAX: 341-7302

❸

SOUTHWEST
LANDSCAPE

48-051 Tyler Street   Chad Skarin
Coachella, California 92236
619-398-6017

4

1

TIMELESS IMAGES

DENNIS R. HOWE
PHOTOGRAPHER

(708) 433

STUDIO OR LOCATION

320 GREENBAY ROAD, HIGHWOOD, IL

H O W E H STUDIOS

2

Lands
Desi
Instal

Mulching,
Edging,
Patios,
Walk

The Gardener
4939 Lower Mountain Road
New Hope, Pennsylvania 18938
------ 215·794·3168 ------

3

1 Design Firm
Teslick Graphics
Designer
Julie L. Teslick
Client
Howe Studios
Photography

2 Design Firm
Full Moon Creations, Inc.
Art Director
Frederic Leleu
Designer
Lisa Leleu
Illustrator
Lisa Leleu
Client
The Gardener
Landscape design and installation

3 Design Firm
Propaganda
Designer
Kagan Atsüren
Client
Self-promotion
Freelance illustration and design

4 Design Firm
Leslie Chan Design Co., Ltd.
Designer
Leslie Chan Wing Kei
Client
Topline Communication Inc.
Production

TASARIM İLLÜSTRASYON   0 · 212 273 18 01

KAGAN ATSÜREN

YAŞARBEY SK. 9/8 80310 MECİDİYEKÖY İSTANBUL

TOPLINE

經典集國際廣告有限公司

4

林 欽 賢 藝術指導
STEVEN LIN Art Director

經典集國際廣告有限公司
台北市敦化南路一段236巷31號 5 樓
TOPLINE COMMUNICATION INC.
5F. No. 31, Lane 236, Tun Hua S. Road, Taipei, Taiwan.
Tel: (02)731-6666 Fax: (02)751-1522

TOD ERNST

Planet Hair

316 267 8000

504 E. DOUGLAS WICHITA KS 67202

Baillie Gerstein

2107 GREENFIELD AVE

LOS ANGELES, CA 90025

TEL. 310.477.5242

FAX. 310.479.7609

ELLEN KNABLE &ASSOC

INCORPORATED

1 2 3 3

SOUTH

LA CIENEGA BLVD.

LOS ANGELES

CALIFORNIA

9 0 0 3 5

TELEPHONE

310 855 8855

F A X

310 657 0265

1 **Design Firm**
Greteman Group
Art Director
Sonia Greteman
Designers
Sonia Greteman, Karen Hogan
Client
Planet Hair
Hair salon

2 **Design Firm**
Jay Vigon Studio
Art Director
Jay Vigon
Designer
Caroline Plasencia
Producer
Caroline Plasencia
Illustrator
Jay Vigon
Client
Baillie Gerstein
Commercial voice-over specialist

3 **Design Firm**
Jay Vigon Studio
Designer
Jay Vigon
Client
Ellen Knable & Associates
Artists' representitive

1

*terri gibbs
photography*

1512

Edison

Suite

100

Dallas

Texas

75207

214

748

6866

2

CENTRE
CHIROPRATIQUE

BLAINVILLE

Pour votre mieux-être

**Dr. Michel Delorme, D.C.
Chiropraticien**

10 boul. de la Seigneurie
Bureau 202
Blainville Québec
J7C 3V5
Tél.: 971.0824

3

Little&AssociatesArchitects

Thomas L. Balke, AIA
Senior Associate

5815 Westpark Drive
Charlotte, NC 28217

Direct Line: 704.561.3414
Facsimile: 704.522.7889
Receptionist: 704.525.6350

4

The
Jones Collection
MANUFACTURERS' REP

Jacqueline L. Jones

TEL (510) 339-1478
FAX (510) 339-7241

5744 GRISBORNE AVE
OAKLAND, CA 94611

5

METROWEST
LANDSCAPE
COMPANY
P.O. Box 874,
Natick,
Massachusetts
01760
"Complete
Landscape
Services"

Eric Meltzer

508.788.0552

617.444.1305

METROWEST

6

SHELLI McCONNELL
Food Writer - Consultant

811 North B Street
Indianola, Iowa 50125

515 - 961 - 9213

1 Design Firm
Sibley/Peteet Design, Inc.
Designer
Derek Welch
Client
Terri Gibbs
Photography

2 Design Firm
D2 Design
Designer
Dominique Duval
Client
Centre Chiropratique Blainville
Chiropractors

3 Design Firm
Mervil Paylor Design
Designer
Mervil M. Paylor
Client
Little & Associates Architects
Commercial architecture

4 Design Firm
Visible Ink
Designer
Sharon Howard Constant
Client
The Jones Collection
Manufacturers' representative

5 Design Firm
SullivanPerkins
Designer
Art Garcia
Client
Metrowest Landscape Company
Landscaping

6 Design Firm
Visual Advantage
Designer
Ann Hiemstra
Client
Shelli McConnell
Food writer and consultant

1

600 CHANEY ST.

LAKE ELSINORE

CALIFORNIA 92530

TEL 714-674-1578

FAX 909-245-2427

1-800-654-1119

2

CHIP LERWICK, *President*

HEARTLAND

SINCE 1993

FUTONS · FIBERS

SAINT LOUIS, MISSOURI

800 239-8022
tel. 314 231-8022
fax 231-8104

*Manufacturers of the
highest-quality
futons, made with a 100%
recycled fiber core.*

*2107 Lucas Avenue
Saint Louis
Missouri 63103*

3

Pitchfork Development, Inc.

Post Office Box 2370

572 Park Avenue

Park City, Utah 84060

Telephone: (801)649-3900

Facsimile: (801)649-3757

James W. Lewis
President

1 Design Firm
Mires Design, Inc.
Art Director
Jose Serrano
Designer
Jose Serrano
Illustrator
Nancy Stahl
Client
Deleo Clay Tile Company
Clay roofing tile retail

2 Design Firm
Phoenix Creative
Art Director
Eric Thoelke
Designer
Eric Thoelke
Client
Heartland Futons
Recycled-fiber futon retail

3 Design Firm
The Weller Institute for
the Cure of Design
Designer
Don Weller
Client
Pitchfork Development Inc.
*Real estate development
and construction*

1 Design Firm
Phoenix Creative
Designer
Ed Mantels-Seeker
Client
Grand Central Post
*Audio and video post-
production facility*

2 Design Firm
Curtis Design
Art Director
David Curtis
Designer
Joan Bittner
Illustrator
Joan Bittner
Client
Valley Sun of California
Sun-dried tomato production

3 Design Firm
Phoenix Creative
Designer
Ed Mantels-Seeker
Client
St. Louis Sports Commission

4 Design Firm
Animus Comunicaçáo
Art Director
Rique Nitzsche
Designers
Rique Nitzsche, Felício Torres
Illustrator
Antonino Homobono
Client
Italia in Bocca
Italian restaurant

1

Kevin DePew
President

Call 314 621.7678
or
Fax 314 621.8800

St. Louis MO 63103

1000 St. Louis Union Station Suite 100

2

Raymond C. Benech
DIRECTOR

VALLEY SUN OF CALIFORNIA

P.O. BOX 549 · 3324 ORESTIMBA ROAD
NEWMAN, CALIFORNIA 95360
TEL: 209.862.1200 · FAX: 209.862.1100

4

MARIA AUGUSTA CIVILETTI

D E L I K A T E S S E N

BARRA FREE SHOPPING, AV. DAS AMÉRICAS, 4.666
LOJA B - 202 GH - BARRA DA TIJUCA - RIO DE JANEIRO
BRASIL - TEL. E FAX: 325 2963 - CEP 22640-102

3

Joe Farrell
Chairman

10 South Broadway
Suite Number 1000
St. Louis, Missouri 63102
314 / 421-4515
Fax / 421-4225

1

Deanie Lenon

A
B
O

A R C H I T E C T S

Abo Architects P.C.

1448 Pennsylvania St.

Denver, Colorado

80203-2012

303.830.0575

FAX.303.830.8930

2

farm fresh
CLARK BROS.
FRUITS & VEGETABLES

Ralph T. Clark

☞ **Office**
5 Concourse Parkway
Suite 3100
Atlanta, Georgia 30328
☎ (404) 804-5830

🌿 **Farm**
Route 6
Moultrie, Georgia 31768
☎ (912) 985-1444

3

Est.1993

MAIN STREET
RESTAURANT

Jeffrey Kadish

446 Columbus Avenue New York, NY 10024 ☎ (212) 873-5025

1 Design Firm
David Warren Design
Designer
David Warren
Client
ABO Architects

2 Design Firm
Coker Golley Ltd.
Art Directors
Jane Coker, Frank Golley
Designer
Julia Mahood
Client
Clark Brothers
Family farms

3 Design Firm
PM Design, Inc.
Designer
Philip Marzo
Client
Main Street Restaurant
American family-style restaurant

❶

Design Firm
Marsh Inc.
Art Director
Greg Conyers
Designer
Greg Conyers
Client
The New American Diner

❷

Design Firm
The Pushpin Group
Art Director
Roxanne Slimak
Designer
Roxanne Slimak
Client
The Portuguese Baking Co.

❸

Design Firm
Gilbert Design
Art Director
Holly Gilbert
Designer
Holly Gilbert
Illustrator
Holly Gilbert
Client
Clarke Brothers Corporate
Catering

❹

Design Firm
Eilts Anderson Tracy
Art Director
Patrice Eilts
Designer
Toni O'Bryan
Illustrator
Patrice Eilts
Client
PB&J Restaurants
Coyote Grill

❺

Design Firm
Leslie Hirst Design Co.
Art Director
Leslie Hirst
Designer
Leslie Hirst
Illustrator
Leslie Hirst
(Hand Lettering)
Client
Good Friends
Baked Goods

❶
Design Firm
Mammoliti Chan Design
Art Director
Tony Mammoliti
Designer
Chwee Kuan Chan
Illustrator
Sebastian Giaccotto,
Chwee Kuan Chan
Client
Essentially Skin Beauty Clinic

❷
Design Firm
Holden & Company
Art Director
Cathe Holden
Designer
Cathe Holden
Illustrator
Cathe Holden
Client
Jennifer Farquhar

1 Design Firm
Peterson & Company
Art Directors
Dave Eliason, Jan Wilson
Designer
Dave Eliason
Illustrator
Bryan L. Peterson
Client
Earth Preserv
*Toiletries, shampoo, and
lotion manufacturing*

2 Design Firm
John Kneapler Design
Designer
John Kneapler
Client
Farm Express Corporation
Fresh produce shipping

3 Design Firm
Visible Ink
Designer
Sharon Howard Constant
Client
Ruth O. Weiss
Personal card

1

earth
preserv

JENNIFER RUPERT
product manager

580 decker drive   suite 204   irving, texas 75062   214-541-8612   fax 214-541-1514

2

Jeffrey M. Siger

Fresh from the farm to you

Farm Express Corporation
107 Hickory Hill Road   Fox Chapel, Pennsylvania 15238
Tel (412) 281-0722   Fax (412) 281-6541

3

BRONX, NEW YORK
AM
28 JUL
1908

(212) 724-8296

RUTH O. WEISS
25 WEST 81ST STREET
NEW YORK, NY 10024

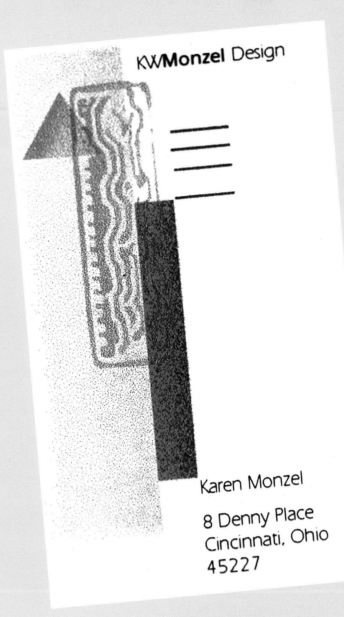

KW Monzel Design

Karen Monzel

8 Denny Place
Cincinnati, Ohio
45227

1 **Design Firm**
KWMonzel Design
Designer
Karen Woods Monzel
Client
Self-promotion
Graphic design

2 **Design Firm**
Linnea Gruber Design
Designer
Linnea Gruber
Client
Self-promotion
Graphic design and advertising

3 **Design Firm**
Adele Bass & Co. Design
Designer
Adele Bass
Client
Sharynn Bass
Advertising copywriter

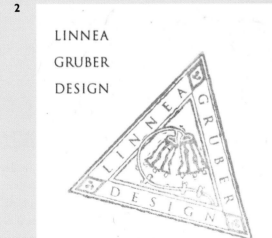

LINNEA
GRUBER
DESIGN

Graphic Design
& Advertising
579 CALLA AVENUE
IMPERIAL BEACH
CALIFORNIA 91932
FAX 429-3347
619-429-3229

SHARYNN BASS

WRITER

161 FOREST LANE

BERKELEY

CALIFORNIA 94708

(510) 526 3906

1

1 Art Director
Vanessa Eckstein
Designer
Vanessa Eckstein
Client
Fernando Arrioja
Mexican filmmaker

2 Design Firm
Tangram Strategic Design
Designer
Antonella Trevisan
Client
Logos Consulenza
*Employment
placement agency*

3 Design Firm
Kaiser Dicken
Art Directors
Debra Kaiser, Craig Dicken
Designer
Debra Kaiser
Illustrator
Debra Kaiser
Client
Brad Rabinowitz
Architect

4 Design Firm
THARP DID IT
Art Director
Rick Tharp
Designers
Amy Bednarek,
Laurie Okamura, Rick Tharp
Client
Self-promotion
*Corporate identity
and brand packaging design*

5 Design Firm
Glazer Graphics
Designer
Nancy Glazer
Client
Self-promotion
Illustration

6 Design Firm
Covi Corporation
Designer
Ursula Loepfe
Client
Self-promotion
Graphic design

FILM MAKER

8 1 8   7 9 2   6 2 4 3

FERNANDO ARRIOJA

628 E CALIFORNIA BLVD

PASADENA

91106 CA

8 1 8   7 9 2   6 2 4 3

2

Antonella Boggio

$1o$

Logos Consulenza
Logos Consulenza s.n.c.
Viale Roma 43a, 28100 Novara
Telefono 0321 459830 R.A.
Fax 0321 458082
Partita IVA 01289840033

3

200 Main Street
Burlington, Vermont 05401
(802) 658-0430

BRAD RABINOWITZ ARCHITECT

Architecture

Space Planning

Interior Design

4

408.354.6726 ⓣ

☎

5

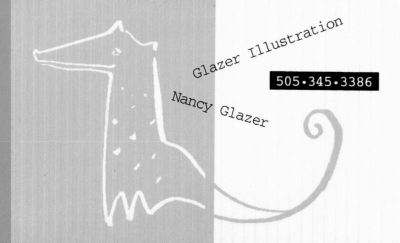
Glazer Illustration

Nancy Glazer

505•345•3386

6

COVI Corporation

USA
5850 OBERLIN DRIVE
SUITE 310
SAN DIEGO, CA 92121
PHONE: 619/481-6566
FAX: 619/792-5426

MONA HOWELL

SWITZERLAND
ROSACKERSTR. 18
CH-4573 LOHN
TEL: 065/47 25 19
FAX: 065/47 26 41

COVI

CORPORATE VISUAL IDENTITY

1

Paperworks design

Graphic Design • Advertising • Photography • Printing

Logos • Brochures • Advertising
Publications • Trade Show Design
Packaging • Environmental Graphics

300 SW Second Street
Corvallis, OR 97333
USA, Planet Earth

503.753.4003
fax 503.754.1006

2

RON ZAHURANEC

PO BOX 65
TUSTIN CA
92681 0065
909 735 7435

Z WORKS

3

R

LEE ANN RHODES
Graphic Designer

⌐105 DUMBARTON RD.
SUITE D
BALTIMORE, MD
21212

1 Design Firm
Paperworks Design
Art Director
Joanne McLennan
Designer
Sue Crawford
Client
Self-promotion
Design

2 Design Firm
Z Works
Designer
Ron Zahuranec
Client
Self-promotion
Graphic design

3 Design Firm
Lee Ann Rhodes Design
Designer
Lee Ann Rhodes
Client
Self-promotion
Graphic design

4 Design Firm
B3 Design
Designer
Barbara B. Breashears
Client
Class Connection
School fund-raising

5 Design Firm
Glazer Graphics
Designer
Nancy Glazer
Client
SongMart Productions
Music publishing

6 Design Firm
Visible Ink
Designer
Sharon Howard Constant
Client
Self-promotion
*Graphic design
and illustration*

4

CLASS CONNECTION

SHARON STOKES
EXECUTIVE VICE PRESIDENT

•

1051 SERPENTINE LANE
PLEASANTON, CA 94566

RING 510/426•6155 FAX 510/426•9797

5

SONG MART
PRODUCTIONS

CHAS YOUNG
14 CASA DEL ORO LOOP
SANTA FE, NM 87505

505 • 466 • 0818

678 13th Street, Suite 202 • Oakland, CA 94612 • TEL (510) 836•4845 • FAX (510) 836•4848

Visible Ink
Graphic Design
Illustration

Sharon Constant

1 Design Firm
Shields Design
Designer
Charles Shields
Client
Camarad, Inc.
Photography

2 Design Firm
K.E. Roehr Design
& Illustration
Designer
K.E. Roehr
Client
Karen Elizabeth, K.E. Roehr
*Handpainted
clothing manufacturing*

3 Design Firm
Jill Tanenbaum Graphic Design
& Advertising, Inc.
Art Director
Jill Tanenbaum
Designer
Catherine Mason
Client
Sarah Kettler
Copywriting

4 Design Firm
Daniel Bastian,
Andreas Weiss
Designers
Daniel Bastian,
Andreas Weiss
Client
Buch & Kunst
Bookstore

5 Design Firm
Greteman Group
Designer
Sonia Greteman
Client
Suzanne Craig
Illustrator representative

1

2

3

4

5

1

2

3

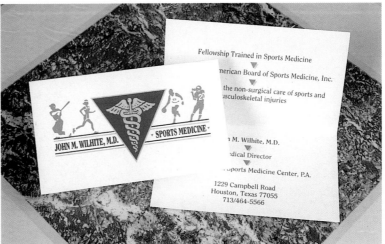

4

1 Design Firm
David Carter Design
Designer
Gary Lobue Jr.
Client
Star Canyon
New Texas cuisine restaurant

2 Design Firm
Susan Northrop Design
Designer
Susan Northrop
Client
Kevin Baker
Landscape and stonescape design

3 Design Firm
MAH Design Inc.
Designer
Mary Anne Heckman
Illustrators
Mary Anne Heckman, Jack Slattery
Client
John M. Wilhite, M.D.
Sports medicine

4 Design Firm
Palmquist & Palmquist Design
Designers
Kurt Palmquist, Denise Palmquist
Illustrator
Kurt Palmquist
Client
Flaming Arrow Lodge
Executive mountain retreat

❶

Design Firm
Gregory Smith Design
Art Director
Gregory L. Smith
Designer
Gregory L. Smith
Illustrator
Norris Peterson
Client
Norris Peterson Illustration

❷

Design Firm
Spirit River Design
Art Director
Steven Pikala
Designer
Steven Pikala
Illustrator
Steven Pikala
Client
Painter's Creek Stables

❸

Design Firm
Qually & Company Inc.
Art Director
Robert Qually
Designer
Robert Qually
Client
Urban American Club

❹

Design Firm
Sayles Graphic Design
Art Director
John Sayles
Designer
John Sayles
Illustrator
John Sayles
Client
The Iowa Group

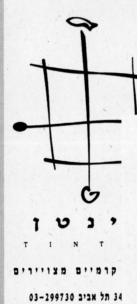

1 Design Firm
The Bradford Lawton
Design Group
Art Directors
Brad Lawton,
Jennifer Griffith-Garcia
Designer
Brad Lawton
Illustrator
Brad Lawton
Client
Dr. Scheel Nayar
Obstetrics and gynecology

2 Design Firm
Peggy Groves Design
Designer
Peggy Groves
Client
Kamehachi Cafe
Late night Japanese restaurant

3 Design Firm
Yaba (Yeh!) Design
Designer
Yael Barnea-Givoni
Client
Self-promotion
Tile design and painting

4 Design Firm
GN Design Studio
Designer
Glenda S. Nothnagle
Client
Dori
*Residential and
commercial cleaning*

DR. SCHEEL NAYAR

OB/GYN

7355 Barlite

San Antonio

Texas 78224

Tel. 210-921-BABY

Fax 210-921-2360

KAMEHACHI
Japanese Restaurant & Sushi Bar

亀
八

1400 North Wells
Chicago, IL 60610
312.664.3663

Dori
Residential & Commercial Cleaning

Voice Mail
&
234-5101

1

FILM & VIDEO
COMMUNICATIONS

MIRA
crea
tive
gr
oup

BOB O'DONNELL
creative director

1200 NW FRONT AVE • SUITE 200

PORTLAND, OREGON 97209

TELE:503•464•0630

FAX:503•464•0782

2

IMPORTER AND REPRESENTATIVE OF AFRICAN
TEXTILES • TRADITIONAL CLOTHINGS • ART • ARTIFACTS
WHOLESALE INQUIRIES WELCOME.

FEMI BANJO
Merchant

78 UPPER A

4765

AFRICAN PRIDE
AT UNDERGROUND ATLANTA

3

PAPER POST

1145 Lindero Canyon Rd., #D3
Thousand Oaks, CA 91362
818•865•0702

4

MARILYN WORSELDINE ♦ MARKET SIGHTS INC
3040 CAMBRIDGE PLACE NORTHWEST WASHINGTON DC 20007
TELEPHONE 202-342-3853 OR FAX 202-337-7851

5

LOS GATOS CYCLERY

FOR THE TOWN
FOR THE TRAIL

THYRA STEVENSON

15954 LOS GATOS BLVD. • LOS GATOS, CA 95032 • FAX 408.356.7092 • TEL 408.356.1644

FOR THE TOWN

1 Design Firm
Oakley Design Studios
Designer
Tim Oakley
Client
Mira Creative Group
Film and video communications

2 Design Firm
Two In Design
Designer
Ed Phelps
Client
African Pride
*Traditional African
merchandise retail*

3 Design Firm
SND, Sue Nan Designs
Designer
Sue Nan Douglass
Client
Paper Post
*Art, rubber stamps
and unusual paper store*

4 Design Firm
Market Sights, Inc
Designer
Marilyn Worseldine
Client
Self-promotion
Graphic design

5 Design Firm
THARP DID IT
Art Director
Rick Tharp
Designers
Laurie Okamura, Rick Tharp
Client
Los Gatos Cyclery
Bicycle retail

1

743 East Lake St.
Wayzata, Minn. 55391
Ph:(612)473-2940

Black's Ford

Ruth Whitney Bowe

1 Design Firm
Tilka Design
Art Director
Jane Tilka
Designer
Anne Koenig
Illustrator
Mike Reed
Client
Black's Ford
Specialty restaurant

2 Design Firm
Robert Bailey Incorporated
Designer
Ellen Bednarek
Client
Ellington Rucksack Co.
*Leather rucksacks, bags,
and wallet manufacturer*

3 Design Firm
Melissa Passehl Design
Designer
Melissa Passehl
Client
Self-promotion
Graphic design

4 Design Firm
Alfred Design
Designer
John Alfred
Client
Self-promotion
Graphic design

5 Design Firm
Melissa Passehl Design
Designer
Melissa Passehl
Client
Glen Rogers Perrotto
Print-making and fine art

2

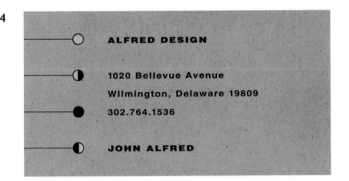

ELLINGTON RUCKSACK CO.

ALECIA ELSASSER

0112 SW Hamilton   Portland, OR 97201
800-736-1222   503-223-7457 tel   503-223-7453 fax

4

○ **ALFRED DESIGN**

◑ 1020 Bellevue Avenue
Wilmington, Delaware 19809

● 302.764.1536

◑ **JOHN ALFRED**

3

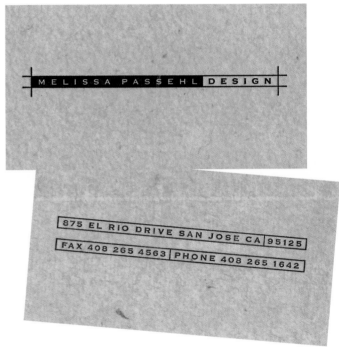

MELISSA PASSEHL DESIGN

875 EL RIO DRIVE SAN JOSE CA 95125

FAX 408 265 4563 | PHONE 408 265 1642

5

glen rogers perrotto

18595 ralya court
cupertino, california
95014

408.446.5401

1

! 212.246.9697 TEL/FAX !

! STRATEGIES

! ART

! EVENTS

! DESIGN

! IMAGE !

340 W 57TH ! SUITE 9A ! NEW YORK, NY 10019 !

INCORPORATED

I.D.E.A.S.

MJ HERSON

PRINCIPAL

73623,503@COMPUSERVE.COM

2

STAN **BAROUH**

PHOTOGRAPHY

704 SLIGO CREEK

PARKWAY

TAKOMA PARK

MARYLAND

2 0 9 1 2

T 202-265-7035

P 202-837-7946

F 202-265-8128

4

117 W 13TH ST #5 NYC 10011

K

KAY WAKABAYASHI

K

212·989·0166

GRAPHIC DESIGN

1 Design Firm
Mo Viele, Inc.
Designer
Mo Viele
Client
I.D.E.A.S.
Communications and design

2 Design Firm
Market Sights, Inc
Designer
Marilyn Worseldine
Illustrator
Norman Ramock
Client
Barouh Photography

3 Design Firm
Tangram Strategic Design
Designer
Enrico Sempi
Client
Mario Finotti
Photography

4 Design Firm
Kay Wakabayashi
Designer
Kay Wakabayashi
Client
Self-promotion
Graphic design

3

MARIO FINOTTI

FOTOGRAFO

VIA XIII MARTIRI 12
28070 GARBAGNA NOVARESE
ITALIA
0321/845192

PARTITA IVA 00408960037
CCIAA NOVARA 128911

1

Steven Abrahams
Landscape Works
207 Dolores Street
San Francisco
CA 94103-2211
Tel. 415.626.8021

2

BLACK SHEEP STUDIO

ILLUSTRATION & DESIGN

NINE WHITE BIRCH ROAD

STANHOPE, NJ 07874

SUSAN MARX
(201) 691-7657

3

BROWNE
PRODUCTION GROUP

————

Eric Browne
3429 Airport Way S.
Seattle, WA 98134
(206) 329-4947
Studio - 382-0591

4

HARRY'S DOVE
Ceramic Sculpture

JENNIFER WALKER
(510) 339-3431

5

good food - good price

Ken Takahashi
(good boy)

the Dog House Waikiki

Sit: King's Village
131 Kaiulani Avenue
Speak:(808) 923-7744
Fetch:(808) 574-2052

1 Design Firm
Barry Power Graphic Design
Designer
Barry Power
Client
Steven Abrahams
Landscape Works
Landscape design

2 Design Firm
Black Sheep Studio
Designer
Susan Marx
Client
Self-promotion
Design and illustration

3 Design Firm
Walsh & Associates, Inc.
Designer
Michael Stearns
Client
Browne Production Group
Photography and film

4 Design Firm
Visible Ink
Designer
Sharon Howard Constant
Client
Harry's Dove
Ceramic sculpture

5 Design Firm
Voice
Designer
Clifford Cheng
Client
The Dog House
Waikiki snack shop

1

Jalal Bassiri
Geschäftsführer

AMADÉ
Reisebüro GmbH
Hauptstraße 91
A-5600 St.Johann / Pg.
Tel.: 0 64 12 / 89 55 - 0
Fax.: 0 64 12 / 89 89

2

NUTRITION

Q U E S T

STEPHANIE S. GREEN
NUTRITION CONSULTANT

3840 CONSTITUTION DR.
DALLAS, TEXAS 75229
2 1 4 - 3 5 7 - 2 7 1 1

3

LA CASA DEL CABRITO

AY-COCULA
MEXICAN RESTAURANT
& CANTINA

JUAN JOSE (PEPE) LOPEZ
GENERAL MANAGER
▲
4010 HWY. 6 SOUTH
HOUSTON, TEXAS 77082
713/531-6800
▲
6707 HARRISBURG
HOUSTON, TEXAS 77011
713/928-2793

CATERING AVAILABLE

4

BACKSTUBE
DIE VOLLKORNBÄCKEREI

Uwe Oeltjenbruns

Friesenstraße 24
30161 Hannover
Tel. (0511) 33 16 72

5

D. Johnson-Jones

Fine Art

Art & Education
Coordinator

Student Center
Southern Illinois University
Carbondale, IL 62901-4407

618.549.2668 (H)
618.453.3636 (W)

6

E N J O Y
T U R I S M O

JOSÉ POPPA

RUA OSCAR FREIRE, 956 1º ANDAR
CEP 01426-000 SÃO PAULO
FONE (011) 883 0663

1 Design Firm
Modelhart Grafik Design
Designer
Herbert O. Modelhart
Client
Amadé
Travel agency

2 Design Firm
Einstein's
Designer
Lonna Morris
Client
Nutrition Quest
Nutrition consulting

3 Design Firm
MAH Design Inc.
Designers
Mary Anne Heckman,
Jack Slattery
Illustrators
Mary Anne Heckman,
Jack Slattery
Client
Ay Cocula Mexican
Restaurant and cantina

4 Design Firm
Anette Kuck-Grafik Design
Designer
Anette Kuck
Client
Backstube
Bakery

5 Design Firm
Purple Seal Graphics
Designer
Lim-Ho Yen
Client
Debra Jones
Fine art and jewelry design

6 Design Firm
Rocha & Yamasaki
Arq.E Design
Designer
Mauricio Rocha
Client
Enjoy Turismo
Brazilian tour agency

1

5600

ADVENTURE 16
OUTDOOR & TRAVEL OUTFITTERS
SINCE 1962

TERRI L. EMBREY

DIRECTOR OF ADVERTISING

ADVENTURE 16, INCORPORATED
4620 ALVARADO CANYON ROAD
SAN DIEGO, CALIFORNIA 92120
TELEPHONE (619) 283-2362 EXT.115
FACSIMILE (619) 283-7956

2

Pat Winterton

Senior Loan Consultant

1730 Minor Avenue
Suite 103
Seattle, WA 98101
Tel: 206/467-8000
Fax: 206/467-6932
Pager: 206/340-7901

4

KEVIN LUONG
PURCHASING ASSISTANT
PILLOW DIVISION

PHONE: (206)624-1057
FAX: (206)625-9783
INTERNET: kevinl@pcf.com

1964 FOURTH AVE. S.
BOX 80385
SEATTLE, WA 98108 USA

3

INTERNATIONAL PRINTING CENTER

JOHN C. REGER
Vice President Marketing

SALES OFFICE
12301 WHITEWATER DRIVE
MINNETONKA, MN 55343
612.933.9765 FAX 612.721.6303

5

ASIAN AMERICAN
HIGHER EDUCATION COUNCIL

Tel: 212.613 9096

Cherokee Station, P.O. Box 20230
New York, NY 10028-0051

1 **Design Firm**
Mires Design, Inc.
Art Director
José Serrano
Designer
José Serrano
Illustrator
Dan Thoner
Client
Adventure 16
Outdoor travel gear retail

2 **Design Firm**
Walsh & Associates, Inc.
Designer
Miriam Lisco
Client
Concord Mortgage
Mortgage company

3 **Design Firm**
Design Center
Art Director
John Reger
Designer
Kobe
Client
International Printing Center
Printing brokerage

4 **Design Firm**
Hornall Anderson Design Works
Art Directors
Jack Anderson, Heidi Favour, Julie Lock
Designer
Leo Raymundo
Illustrator
Carolyn Vibbert
Client
Pacific Coast Feather Company
Down-feather products manufacturing

5 **Design Firm**
Chee Wang Ng
Designer
Chee Wang Ng
Client
Asian American
Higher Education Council

❶

Design Firm
Leah Lococo
Designer
Leah Lococo
Client
Leah Lococo

❷

Design Firm
Blind Mice
Art Director
Erick Ruffing
Designer
Erick Ruffing
Client
Mary Wilson Photography

❸

Design Firm
Planet Design Co.
Art Director
Planet Design Co.
Designer
Planet Design Co.
Client
Rebholz Photographers

❹

Design Firm
Gable Design Group
Art Director
Tony Gable
Designers
Tony Gable, Jana S. Nishi
Client
Gable Design Group

❺

Design Firm
Murrie Lienhart Rysner &
Associates
Art Director
Kate McSherry
Designer
Kate McSherry
Client
Rung Photography

❶

Design Firm
Qually & Company Inc.
Art Director
Robert Qually
Designer
Robert Qually
Illustrator
Bob Ziering
Client
Associated Piping &
Engineering Co.

❷

Design Firm
Tim Harris Design
Art Director
Tim Harris, Alan Disparte
Designers
Alan Disparte, Tim Harris
Illustrator
Alan Disparte
Client
Urban Eyes Optometry

❸

Design Firm
Morla Design
Art Director
Jennifer Morla
Designers
Jennifer Morla, Craig Bailey
Illustrator
Craig Bailey
Client
Ristorante Ecco

❹

Design Firm
Komarow Design
Art Director
Ronni Komarow
Designer
Ronni Komarow
Illustrator
Julia Talcott
Client
Komarow Design

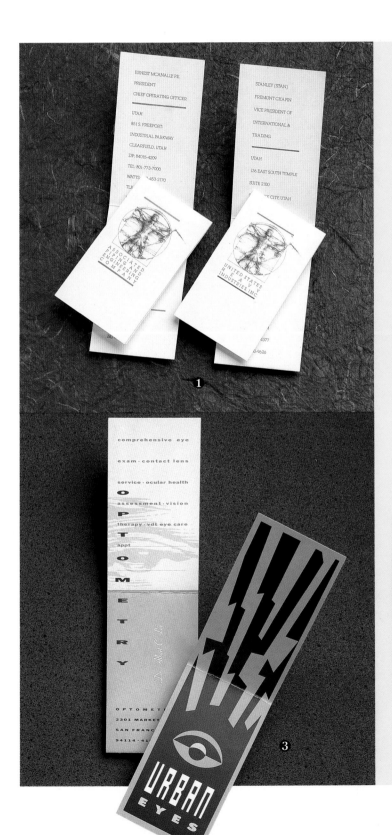

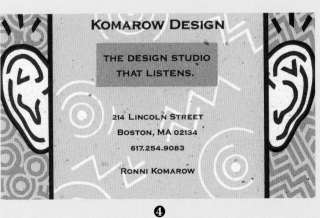

I

Visual Artist
Joan C. Hollingswor[th]
2824 NE 22 • Portland, Oregon
(503) 287-6439

2

LORI ANZALONE
illustration

35-02 BERDAN AVE FAIR LAWN NJ 07410
201-796-5588/5960 • FAX 201-796-2698

1 Design Firm
Joan C. Hollingsworth
Designer
Joan C. Hollingsworth
Client
Self-promotion
Visual artist

2 Design Firm
Lori Anzalone
Designer
Lori Anzalone
Client
Self-promotion
Illustration

3 Design Firm
Squeak
Designer
Robin Dick
Client
Self-promotion
Design and illustration

4 Design Firm
Propaganda
Designer
Kagan Atsüren
Client
Self-promotion
Advertising and design

5 Design Firm
Dennis Irwin Illustration
Art Director
Andrew Danish
Designer
Dennis Irwin
Illustrator
Dennis Irwin
Client
Self-promotion
Illustration

3

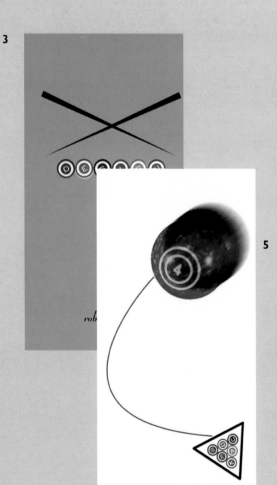

rob

4

Olcay ÖZDEMİR

Propaganda Tanıtım ve Tasarım. İnönü Cad. Ongan Apartmanı 53/13 34504 Ayazpaşa / Taksim
Telefon. 0 - 212 - 243 63 10 / 0 - 212 - 243 66 34 Faks. 0 - 212 - 244 27 02

5

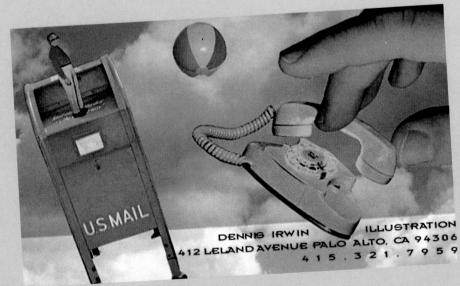

DENNIS IRWIN   ILLUSTRATION
412 LELAND AVENUE PALO ALTO. CA 94306
415 . 321 . 7959

1 Design Firm
Fullmoon Creations, Inc.
Art Director
Frederic Leleu
Designer
Lisa Leleu
Illustrator
Lisa Leleu
Client
Ed Marco—Photography

2 Design Firm
Design Center
Art Director
John Reger
Designer
Kobe
Client
Station Nineteen
Architecture

3 Design Firm
Greteman Group
Art Director
Sonia Greteman
Designers
Sonia Greteman, Karen Hogan
Client
Jake's Attic
Children's science television program

4 Design Firm
Pinkhaus Design Corp.
Designer
Claudia De Castro
Client
Entertainment Agents, Inc.
Entertainment production

5 Design Firm
Sayles Graphic Design
Designer
John Sayles
Client
Western Regional
Greek Conference

1

ED MARCO
PHOTOGRAPHY
1530 LOCUST ST.
SUITE 3
PHILA. PA 19102
215•789•3006

2

STATION NINETEEN
ARCHITECTS, INC.

DARREL LeBARRON,
PART

2001 UNIVERSITY
AVENUE SOUTHEAST
MINNEAPOLIS,
MINNESOTA 55414

612.623.1800
FAX 623.0012

ARCHITECTS,
PLANNERS,
INTERIORS

3

P.O. Box #781714
Wichita, KS 67278
Tel 316 685 3955
Fax 316 687 9477
Steve Jacobs

JAKE'S ATTIC

4

305•666•1363 FAX 305•665•7249

RONNIE FRIEDMAN

ENTERTAINMENT AGENTS, INC.
P.O. BOX
43•1045
MIAMI
FLORIDA
33243

5

WRGC
3 1 5 1
UNIVERSITY
CENTER
CAMP
ACTIVI
CENT
UNIVERS
CALIFOR
SANTA BA
SANTA BARBARA,

WESTERN REGIONAL
GREEK CONFERENCE

1 Design Firm
Julia Tam Design
Designer
Julia Chong Tam
Client
Self-promotion
Graphic design

2 Design Firm
Sibley/Peteet Design, Inc.
Designer
Derek Welch
Client
Sean McCormick
Photography

3 Design Firm
Lorna Stovall Design
Designer
Lorna Stovall
Client
Land, Rock & Water
Landscape design

4 Design Firm
Jeff Labbé Design 0950
Designer
Jeff Labbé
Client
Performance group
Printing

5 Design Firm
Willoughby Design Group
Designer
Debbie Friday
Client
Atwood & Associates
Market research

6 Design Firm
ifx Visual Marketing
Designer
James F. Stone Jr.
Client
Self-promotion
Advertising

1
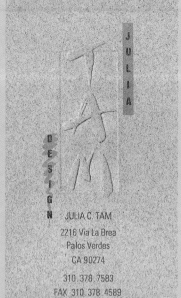

2

Sean
McCORMICK
Photographer
5349
Amesbury
#103
Dallas
TX
75206
214·691·9332

3
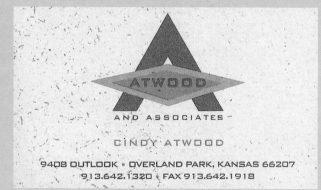

MARTIN C. HURST
LAND, ROCK & WATER
LANDSCAPE CONSTRUCTION
P.O. Box 117461
BURLINGAME, Ca 94011
(415) 578-3801
CONTRACTORS LICENCE #654478

5
ATWOOD
AND ASSOCIATES
CINDY ATWOOD
9408 OUTLOOK • OVERLAND PARK, KANSAS 66207
913.642.1320 • FAX 913.642.1918

6

JAMES F. STONE JR.
ifx
VISUAL MARKETING
GRAPHIC DESIGN
SILK SCREENING
EMBROIDERY
SIGNS / BANNERS
166 E. Broadway
Atwater, CA 95301
Tel 209•357•8578
Fax 209•357•7535
800•789•8870

4

PERFORMANCE GROUP
from ideas
to ink
michael p. rucinski
certified forms consultant
five hundred
harrington st. unit a-2
corona, california
zip code 91720
PH [800] 846-7468
PH [909] 273-7390
FX [909] 273-7395

1

CAVU MANAGEMENT INC.

PO Box 3841
Aspen, CO 81612
303.925.2432

JEFF FRIDAY

PRESIDENT/CHIEF PILOT

C A V U

2

Pavé

DONNA L. EDELSON
Jewelry Designer

· · · · ·

1128 MONTANA AVE.
SANTA MONICA, CA 90403
TEL 310/458-3492
FAX 310/394-3226

3

Team 7
International

Architecture
Interior Design
Planning

Ronald Lee
Director

李中興
總監

TEAM
7
INTERNATIONAL

1011 Kearny Street
San Francisco
CA 94133
415 986.8877
FAX 415 391.5513

4

801 East Lincoln
Wichita, KS 67211
(316) 267.2244
Fax (316) 267.0559

Kathy Anderson   a not-for-profit agency

Customer Service

WICHITA INDUSTRIES & SERVICES FOR THE BLIND, INC.

5

Gourmet C
Weddings
Parties
Holiday Events
Meetings
Grand Openings
Special Events

the
ESPRESSO
GOURMET

"Coffee Catering
for Elegant Affairs"

Julie R. Smith
President

P.O. Box 2281

La Jolla

California 92038

Tel. (619) 541.7822

1 Design Firm
Willoughby Design Group
Designer
Debbie Friday
Client
CAVU Management Inc.
Airplane management

2 Design Firm
Shimokochi/Reeves
Art Directors
Mamoru Shimokochi,
Anne Reeves
Designer
Mamoru Shimokochi
Client
Pavé
Jewelry retail

3 Design Firm
Julia Tam Design
Designer
Julia Chong Tam
Client
Team 7 International
Architectual firm

4 Design Firm
Greteman Group
Designers
Sonia Greteman,
Bill Gardner
Client
Witchita Industries &
Services for the Blind, Inc.

5 Design Firm
Steven Morris Design
Designer
Steven Morris
Client
The Espresso Gourmet
Gourmet coffee catering

1 **Design Firm**
Vibeke Nodskov
Designer
Vibeke Nodskov
Client
Groupvision (Nordic)

2 **Design Firm**
Blue Sky Design
Designer
Maria Dominguez
Client
Nicole Bailey
Design consulting

3 **Design Firm**
Catalina Communications
Designer
Marji Keim-López
Client
Self-promotion
Environmental graphic design

4 **Design Firm**
Becker Design
Designer
Neil Becker
Illustrator
Deborah Hernandez
Client
Instinct Art Gallery

1

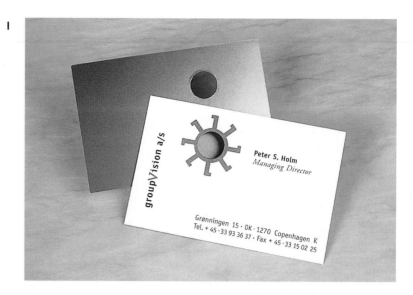

2

3

4

1

Pete LaSalle

Illustration & Design

708·695·9971

2

TOM CUTTS

A PARADE OF FANTASY AND IMAGINATION

(510) 832-0714

Intimate, memorable
gatherings...created
in the warmth of
your home.

Call Marco with your
special requests. Select
from a broad range of
pricing, menu sugges-
tions and entertainment
th
ir!

20

98008

3

MARCO PELLEGRINI

Italian Caterer

Live The Romance
Of Italy...

4

Robin Lipner Digital
220 West 21st St. 2E New York, NY 10011
Phone:929-5807   Fax: 229-1674   email: binx2@panix.com

1 Design Firm
LaSalle Illustration & Design
Designer
Pete LaSalle
Client
Self-promotion
Illustration and design

2 Design Firm
Visible Ink
Designer
Sharon Howard Constant
Client
Tom Cutts
Magician

3 Design Firm
Price Learman Associates
Designer
Ross West
Client
Marco Pellegrini
Italian food catering

4 Design Firm
Robin Lipner Digital
Designer
Robin Lipner
Client
Self-promotion
Illustration, animation, imaging,
and retouching

5 Design Firm
Damion Hickman Design
Designer
Damion Hickman
Client
Napa Valley Gourmet Salsa
Manufacturing Company

5

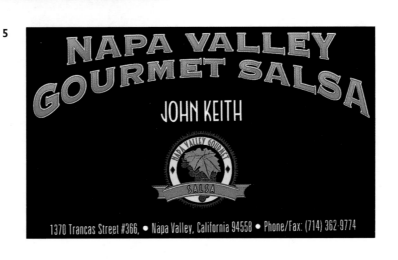

NAPA VALLEY GOURMET SALSA

JOHN KEITH

1370 Trancas Street #366, • Napa Valley, California 94558 • Phone/Fax: (714) 362-9774

❶

Design Firm
Mervil Paylor Design
Designer
Mervil M. Paylor
Client
Johnson-Powell

❷

Design Firm
Studio MD
Art Directors
Jesse Doquillo, Randy Lim,
Glenn Mitsui
Designer
Jesse Doquillo, Randy Lim,
Glenn Mitsui
Illustrator
Glenn Mitsui
Client
Colaizzo Opticians

❸

Design Firm
McMonigle & Spooner
Designer
Stan Spooner
Client
Foremost Packaging

❹

Design Firm
Eric Roinestad Design
Art Director
Eric Roinestad
Designer
Eric Roinestad
Client
Claudine Blackwell

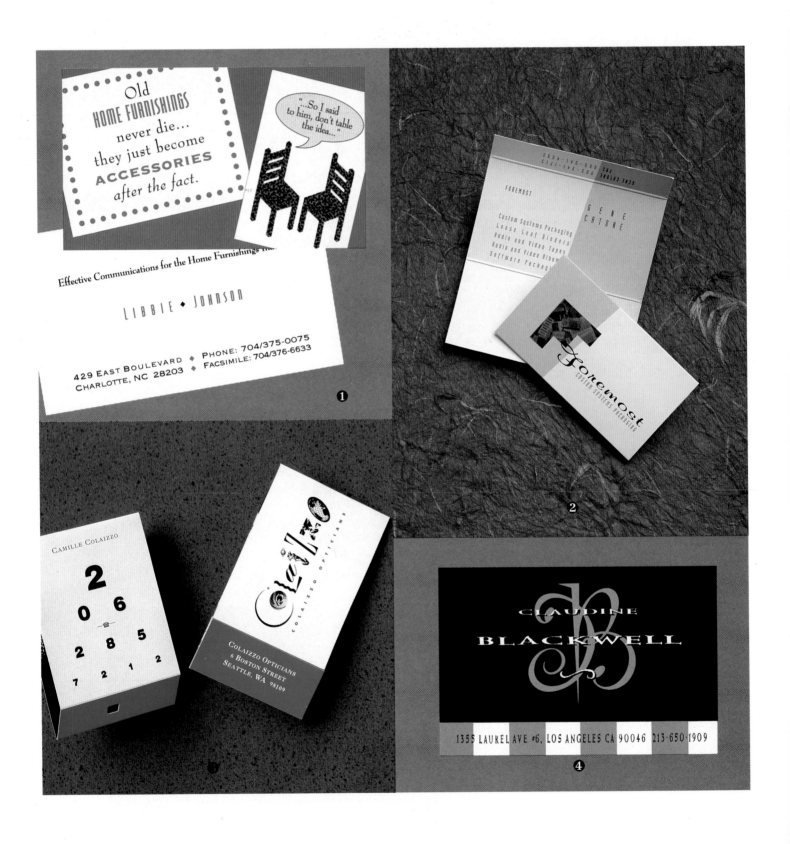

❶

Design Firm
Blind Mice
Art Director
Eric Ruffing
Designer
Eric Ruffing
Client
Blind Mice

❷

Design Firm
Pinkhaus Design Corp.
Art Directors
Joel Fuller, Mark Cantor
Designer
Tom Sterlin

❸

Design Firm
Spirit River Design
Art Director
Steven Pikala
Designer
Steven Pikala
Illustrator
Steven Pikala
Client
Spirit River Design

❹

Design Firm
THARP DID IT
Designer
Rick Tharp, Colleen Sullivan,
Sandy Russell
Client
Stoddard's Brewhouse
& Eatery

❶

❷

❸

❹

I

JALBERT
RASNACK
ANGLIN

ARCHITECTURE
INTERIOR DESIGN

THOMAS J. RASNACK
PRINCIPAL

SUITE 1900
1218 THIRD AVE.
SEATTLE, WA 98101
FAX (206) 682

(206) 467.9

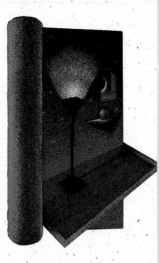

200 CALLECITA PL. - B • SANTA FE, NEW MEXICO 87501 • 505.984.0688

LESLIE HARRELL DILLEN
ACTRESS / PLAYWRIGHT

LESLIE HARRELL DILLEN
ACTRESS / PLAYWRIGHT

200 CALLECITA PL. - B
SANTA FE, NEW MEXICO 87501
505.984.0688

2

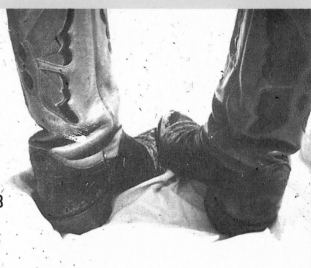

LESLIE
HARRELL
DILLEN

ACTRESS / PLAYWRIGHT

200 CALLECITA PL. - B
SANTA FE, NM 87501
505.984.0688

1 Design Firm
Michael Courtney Design
Designer
Michael Courtney
Illustrators
Michael Courtney,
Jonathan Coombs, Gary Jacobsen
Client
Jalbert/Rasnack/Angun
Architecture

2 Design Firm
Cisneros Design
Art Director
Fred Cisneros
Designer
Fred Cisneros
Photographer
Leslie Harrell Dillen
Client
Leslie Harrell Dillen
Actress and playwright

1

MEN at WORK

DALE RICH
PROPRIETOR
375-2316
PAGER NO.
383-7569

2

Margaret Fisher

CREATIVE
OPTIONS
IN
MARKETING
PROMOTIONS

PH 075 75 5297

3/129
SUNSHINE BLV
MERMAID WATERS
QLD 4218

3

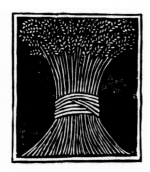

KAMEHACHI café

1400 NORTH WELLS ▸ SECOND FLOOR
CHICAGO IL 60610

TEL. 312-664-1361
TUESDAY - SUNDAY UNTIL 2:00 AM

FOR LATE NIGHT
SUSHI & SPIRITS

4

JANET MILLER
Food Stylist
Home Economist

310·459·9139

5

GREG STEWART

EVOLUTION

FILM & TAPE, INC.

5358 CARTWRIGHT AVENUE

NORTH HOLLYWOOD, CA 91601

PHONE:818.505.0333 FAX:818.505.1333

1 Design Firm
The Woldring Company
Designer
Robert Woldring
Client
Dale Rich
Home maintenance and repair

2 Design Firm
Veronica Graphic Design
Designer
Veronica Tasnadi
Client
Margaret Fisher
Marketing and promotion

3 Design Firm
Peggy Groves Design
Designer
Peggy Groves
Client
Kamehachi Cafe
Late night Japanese restaurant

4 Design Firm
Sage Brush Design
Designer
Danielle Bewer
Client
Janet Miller
Food stylist

5 Design Firm
Lorna Stovall Design
Designer
Lorna Stovall
Client
Evolution Film & Tape

1

PACIFIC
WORD PROCESSING

P E G G Y   W A L K E R

1831 UNION STREET
SAN FRANCISCO, CA. 94123
415/346-2898

2

AISA REYES

AISA REYES DESIGNS
920 SAN JOSE ST., IDI VILLAGE, PARAÑAQUE, M.M.
8243958 ● EC PAGER # 230163

3

TILKA
D E S I G N

1422 West La
Suite 314
Minneapolis,
55408-2656

CARLA SCHOLZ MUELLER   612 . 822.64
Graphic Designer   612 . 822.6

TILKA
D E S I G N

1400 West Lake Street
Suite 314
Minneapolis, Minnesota
55408

JANE TILKA   612 . 822.6422
Graphic Designer   612 . 822.6929 fax

TILKA
D E S I G N

1400 West Lake Street
Suite 314
Minneapolis, Minnesota
55408

CARLA SCHOLZ MUELLER   612 . 822.6422
Graphic Designer   612 . 822.6929 fax

1 Design Firm
B3 Design
Designer
Barbara B. Breashears
Client
Pacific Word Processing

2 Design Firm
Aisa Reyes Design
Designer
Aisa Reyes
Client
Self-promotion
Design studio

3 Design Firm
Tilka Design
Art Director
Jane Tilka
Designer
Brad Hartman
Client
Self-promotion
Graphic design

4 Design Firm
Jerry Cowart Designers Inc.
Designer
Jerry Cowart
Client
Al Fresco Trattoria
Restaurant

4

ALFRESCO
TRATTORIA

Beppe Berti
Donna Berti

217 STATE STREET
SANTA BARBARA • CALIFORNIA 93101
■ 805●963●1370

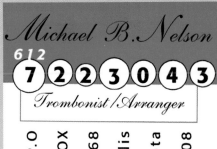

Michael B.Nelson

612

7 2 2 3 0 4 3

Trombonist / Arranger

P.O BOX 80568
Minneapolis Minnesota 55408

Bone 2B WILD

MUSIC

young &. Lynch
DESIGN

Donna M. Young
Creative Director

1328 Emerald Street
San Diego, California
92109

Voice/Facsimile
619.270.4214

COSMETIC

EVITA

MEDIZINISCHE FUSSPFLEGE
PARFUMERIE

ANNETTE SCHÖNLECHNE
A-6793 GASCHURN NR.3 TELEFON 055 58/87 1

BANKKAUFFRAU:

ANJA SCHINDELWICK

Wollen Sie diese Bank kaufen?

**GLUCKENSTEINWEG 86
61350 BAD HOMBURG**

TEL 06172 - 3 77 05

MUAI

MARKETING STRATEGIES
PRODUCT DEVELOPMENT

Melinda Dworkin
President

312.761.9855

7141 North Kedzie, Suite 413
Chicago, Illinois 60645
fax 312.761.9856

1 Design Firm
Stress Lab
Designer
Lizz Luce
Client
Mike Nelson
Trombonist

2 Design Firm
Young & Lynch Design
Designer
Donna M. Young
Client
Self-promotion
Graphic design

3 Design Firm
Grafik Design Ganahl Christoph
Designer
Ganahl Christoph
Client
Annette Schonlechner
Cosmetic consulting

4 Design Firm
Tandem Design
Designer
Caren Schindelwick
Client
Anja Schindelwick
Financial advising

5 Design Firm
Bakagai Design
Designer
Michael M. Hammerman
Client
MDAI
*Marketing and
product development*

1

Stephen Wasserberger

WASSERBERGER BENSON
PARTNERSHIP, ARCHITECTS PC

1220 S.W. Morrison

Suite 900

Portland, Oregon 97205

Tel. 503-228-2511

FAX 503-228-6839

2

714.650.9464
FAX 714.650.9470
ALEEDA WETSUITS
869 WEST 15TH ST. UNIT A
NEWPORT BEACH, CA
92663

3

Ann Indykiewicz
Sales & Marketing Assistant

Schmidt Printing Inc.
1101 Frontage Rd. N.W., Byron, MN 55920
507 775-6400 fax 507 775-6655

schmidt

4

JACK WILLIAMS
Creative Planning & Execution

ASTRA MERCK

725 Chesterbrook Blvd.
Wayne, PA 19087-5677
610 695-1442
Fax 610 889-1287

1 Design Firm
Robert Bailey Incorporated
Designer
Dan Franklin
Client
The Wasserberger
Benson Partnership
Architecture

2 Design Firm
13th Floor
Designer
Eric Ruffing
Client
Aleeda Wetsuits
Surfing gear design

3 Design Firm
MC Studio/Times
Mirror Magazines
Art Director
Paul Kelly
Designers
Paul Kelly, Monica Götz
Client
Schmidt Printing

4 Design Firm
Peterson Blyth Pearson
Art Director
Ronald A. Peterson
Designer
Amy Happ
Client
Astra Merck
Pharmaceutical company

5 Design Firm
Brainstorm Design
Designer
Bob Downs
Client
Self-promotion
Graphic design

5

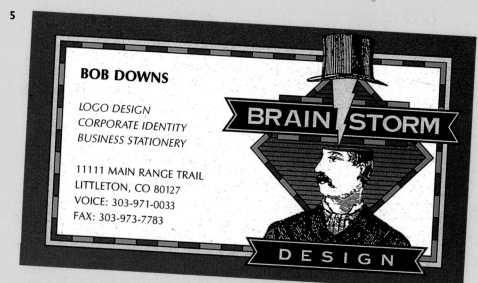

BOB DOWNS

LOGO DESIGN
CORPORATE IDENTITY
BUSINESS STATIONERY

11111 MAIN RANGE TRAIL
LITTLETON, CO 80127
VOICE: 303-971-0033
FAX: 303-973-7783

BRAINSTORM

DESIGN

1

Dr. Manuel Sy Women's Health Center 施 純 泰 婦 產 中 心

Daily 12 noon to 6 p.m.

Manuel C. Sy, M.D.
Obstetrics and Gynecology

110 Lafayette Street, 7th. Floor
New York, NY 10013-4116

Dr. Manuel Sy Women's Health Center 施 純 泰 婦 產 中 心

每日中午十二時至下午六時

施 純 泰 醫學博士

手術專科
婦產科

紐約市華埠拉菲逸街一一零號七樓
電話 : 212. 274 8088 • 傳真 : 212. 274 0880

2

CAMBRIDGE
FRIENDS SCHOOL

Nelda L. Barrón
Director of Admission

5 Cadbury Road
Cambridge, Massachusetts 02140
{617} 354 3880
{617} 876 1815 facsimile

3

SANDIS DESIGNS
BAUBLES & BEADS
Sandi Wasserstein

415.454.0731

20 Locksly Lane . San Rafael, CA 94901

4

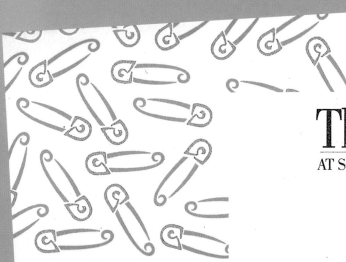

TheBirthPlace
AT SOUTHWEST GENERAL HOSPITAL

Bonnie Jimenez
Perinatal Education Coordinator

7400 Barlite • San Antonio, TX 78224 • (210) 921-8682 • Fax (210) 921-8629

1 Design Firm
Chee Wang Ng
Designer
Chee Wang Ng
Client
Dr. Manuel Sy Women's
Health Center

2 Design Firm
Marc English Design
Designer
Marc English
Client
Cambridge Friends School
Quaker school

3 Design Firm
Sunny Shender Design
Designer
Sunny Shender
Client
Sandis Designs
Fine jewelry and beadwork retail

4 Design Firm
The Bradford Lawton Design Group
Art Directors
Brad Lawton, Jennifer Griffith-Garcia
Designer
Brad Lawton
Illustrator
Jody Laney
Client
The BirthPlace at
Southwest General Hospital
Birthing center

1 Design Firm
13th Floor
Designer
Eric Ruffing
Client
Cyan Video Production
Music and video production

2 Design Firm
Blue Sky Design
Designers
Robert Little, Joanne Little,
Maria Dominguez
Client
Self-promotion
Graphic design

3 Design Firm
Peat Jariya Design/Metal Studio
Art Director
Peat Jariya
Designer
Peat Jariya Design Staff
Client
Self-promotion
Graphic design

4 Design Firm
13th Floor
Designer
Eric Ruffing
Client
Susan Frank & David Frisch
Furniture design and fabrication

5 Design Firm
Marise Mizrahi
Designer
Marise Mizrahi
Client
Self-promotion
Consulting

1

[c y a n]

STEVE CRIST

4 4 7 0
SUNSET BLVD
SUITE 300
LOS ANGELES
CALIFORNIA
9 0 0 2 7

FAX 213 481 1900
TEL 213 481 2500

2

BLUE SKY DESIGN

JOANNE C. LITTLE
Vice President & Creative Director

10300 Sunset Drive, Suite 353, Miami, Florida 33173
Telephone 305·271·2063 Facsimile 305·271·2064

3

[metal] Studio Inc. 13164 Memorial Drive #222, Houston, Texas 77079

Peat Jariya

[metal]

713.523.5177

4

furniture
DESIGN
fabrication
SUSAN FRANK + DAVID FRISCH
1928 echo park av, los angeles, ca 90026
TEL. 213. FAX 213.644.0496
644.0495

5

Design
Art

Marise Mizrahi

274.8663
212.

74 Leonard St. #6A New York, NY 10013

Photography

1

SHIMOKOCHI/REEVES

ANNE REEVES
PRINCIPAL

PHONE: 213 937 3414   4465 WILSHIRE BLVD., SUITE 100   FAX: 213 937 3417
LOS ANGELES, CA 90010-3704

2

Paul Mühl GmbH

Telefon 089/91 51 87

Entwicklungen
von Verpackungen,
Displays, Werbemitteln
und Musterbau

Höslstraße 22
81927 München
Fax 089/910 18 79

3

HT **DR. HANS TIEFENBACHER**
WIRTSCHAFTSTREUHÄNDER · STEUERBERATER
A-5600 ST. JOHANN I. PG., HAUPTSTRASSE 26,
TEL. (0 64 12) 56 56-0, FAX (0 64 12) 56 56 16

4

CALIFORNIA **SKI** COMPANY

DANIEL WINTER

CALIFORNIA SKI COMPANY
843 GILMAN STREET, BERKELEY, CA 94710
RING 510/527-6411 FAX 510/526-0547

5

Brad Carlton
GUITARIST

All styles.
More than 24 years
of teaching and
professional playing.

Staff Guitarist and
Educational Director
for NOTES ON CALL.

813 381.1066

6

VONTRESS

1015 Washington Ave

Number 402

St Louis Missouri 63101

314 231 8988

FAX 314 231 8988

---

1 Design Firm
Shimokochi/Reeves
Art Directors
Mamoru Shimokochi,
Anne Reeves
Designer
Mamoru Shimokochi
Client
Self-promotion
Graphic design

2 Design Firm
Tandem Design
Designer
Caren Schindelwick
Client
Paul Mühl GmbH
*Product design, packaging,
and display*

3 Design Firm
Modelhart Grafik Design
Designer
Herbert O. Modelhart
Client
Dr. Hans Tiefenbacher
Tax consulting

4 Design Firm
B3 Design
Designer
Barbara B. Breashears
Client
California Ski Company
Retail ski shop

5 Design Firm
Ken Weightman Design
Designer
Ken Weightman
Client
Brad Carlton
Guitarist

6 Design Firm
Phoenix Creative
Designer
Eric Thoelke
Client
Von Tress
Architects

1

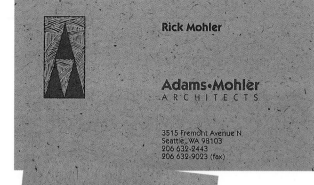

Rick Mohler

Adams•Mohler
ARCHITECTS

3515 Fremont Avenue N.
Seattle, WA 98103
206 632-2443
206 632-9023 (fax)

Adams•Mohler
ARCHITECTS

2

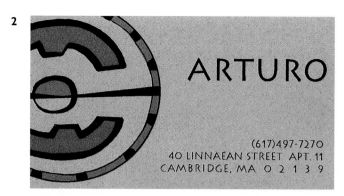

ARTURO

(617)497-7270
40 LINNAEAN STREET APT. 11
CAMBRIDGE, MA 0 2 1 3 9

3

A DIVISION OF CONSOLIDATED MANAGEMENT CO.

2894 106TH STREET SUITE 104

DES MOINES, IOWA 50322

OFFICE PHONE: (515) 278-9774

HOME PHONE: (303) 936-3827

MIKE ANDERSON

DIRECTOR OF CAMP SERVICES

1 Design Firm
Robert Williamson
Designer
Robert Williamson
Client
Adams-Mohler
Architecture

2 Design Firm
Karyl Klopp Design
Designer
Karyl Klopp
Client
Arturo
Holistic counseling

3 Design Firm
Sayles Graphic Design
Designer
John Sayles
Client
Hungry Camper
Resort food service

4 Design Firm
Cisneros Design
Designer
Fred Cisneros
Client
Custom Properties of Santa Fe
*Commercial and
residential building*

4

CARLA HILEY
office manager

CUSTOM PROPERTIES
OF SANTA FE
...a general contracting firm

1494 St. Francis Drive
Santa Fe, New Mexico 87501
505-982-8824
FAX: 505-989-3669

1

Coffee, Tea
Espresso & Gifts

Ross Davidson

510-339-8187
5772 Thornhill Drive
Oakland, CA 94611

2

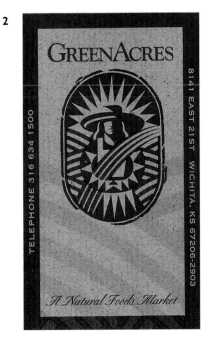

GreenAcres

TELEPHONE 316 634 1500

8141 EAST 21ST · WICHITA, KS 67206-2903

A Natural Foods Market

3

MICHAEL ABELL
322 SO. BROADWAY
WICHITA, KANSAS
ZIP 67202 4304
TEL 316 263 6939
FAX 316 265 0081

ABELL PEARSON
PRINTING COMPANY

1 Design Firm
Visible Ink
Designer
Sharon Howard Constant
Client
Albuquerque Connection
Coffee house

2 Design Firm
Greteman Group
Designer
Sonia Greteman
Client
Green Acres
Natural foods market

3 Design Firm
Greteman Group
Designer
Sonia Greteman
Client
Abell Pearson
Printing

4 Design Firm
THARP DID IT
Art Director
Rick Tharp
Designers
Laurie Okamura, Rick Tharp
Illustrators
Jana Heer, Laurie Okamura
Client
Los Gatos Bar and Grill

5 Design Firm
B3 Design
Designer
Barbara B. Breashears
Client
Apple Lane Baker

4

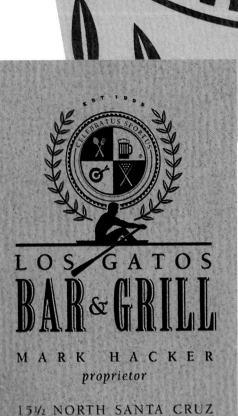

LOS GATOS
BAR & GRILL

MARK HACKER
proprietor

15½ NORTH SANTA CRUZ
LOS GATOS, CALIFORNIA 95030
TELEFAX 408.366.2222
TELEPHONE 408.399.LGBG

5

GOURMET FRUIT TARTS

APPLE, CHERRY,
PUMPKIN, LEMON,
STRAWBERRY / RHUBARB
IN SEASON

▼

SUGAR FREE
WHEAT FREE
LOW CHOLESTEROL
LOW FAT
ELEGANT AND DELICIOU

▼

LYNDA BROCKMANN
PRESIDENT

121 PONDEROSA LANE
WALNUT CREEK, CA 94595
RING 510/932-8283
FAX 510/935-8934

1

Milestones

Edmond Sabet
President

1965 Tubeway Avenue

Los Angeles , CA

90040

(213) 890-0876

FAX (213) 728-4221

2

**14814 Heritage Wood Drive
Houston, Texas 77082-4115**
▼   713·558·2246   ▼
Fax Number 713·589·8580

3

Mizrahi **Jacky**

Via L. Tolstoi 106
Milano 20146 Italy
Fax 02.425.759
*Tel.*02.422.4712
Cel. 0336.395.324

5

**WHITE HOUSE CONFERENCE
ON TRAVEL AND TOURISM**
1440 NEW YORK AVENUE, NW
WASHINGTON, DC 20005
202-501-8140 USTTA TELEPHONE
202-637-1230 TELEPHONE
202-637-9354 FACSIMILE
LORANNE E. AUSLEY
EXECUTIVE DIRECTOR

1 Design Firm
Julia Tam Design
Designer
Julia Chong Tam
Client
Milestones Greeting Card Co.

2 Design Firm
MAH Design Inc.
Designer
Mary Anne Heckman
Illustrator
Jack Slattery
Client
Jack Slattery Illustrator

3 Design Firm
Marise Mizrahi
Designer
Marie Mizrahi
Client
Self-promotion

4 Design Firm
Eat Design
Art Director
Patrice Eilts-Jobe
Designers
Patrice Eilts-Jobe, Toni O'Bryan
Illustrators
Patrice Eilts, Toni O'Bryan
Client
Lakemary Center
Mental disabilities facility

5 Design Firm
Market Sights, Inc.
Designer
Marilyn Worseldine
Client
White House Conference
on Travel and Tourism

4

LAKEMARY
CENTER

WILLIAM R. CRAIG, PH.D.
PRESIDENT

100 LAKEMARY DRIVE

PAOLA, KS 66071

913-294-4361   FAX 913-294-4910

❶

Design Firm
Christine Haberstock
Illustration
Art Director
Christine Haberstock
Designer/Illustrator
Christine Haberstock
Client
Shebeen Management

❷

Design Firm
Dean Johnson Design
Art Director
Jerry Velasco
Designer
Jerry Velasco
Illustrator
Jerry Velasco
Client
The Bungalow Inc.

❸

Design Firm
Pont Street Inc.
Art Director
Christ Pinkham
Designer
Chris Pinkham
Illustrator
Chris Pinkham
Client
Deborah Hoffman

❹

Design Firm
Gable Design Group
Art Director
Tony Gable
Designer
Tony Gable
Illustrator
Karin Yamagiwa
Client
Jeffrey Ross Music

❺

Design Firm
O'Leary Illustration
Art Director
Patty O'Leary
Designer
Patty O'Leary
Illustrator
Patty O'Leary
Client
O'Leary Illustration

❻

Design Firm
Graphicus Corporation
Art Director
Micah Piccirilli
Designer
Micah Piccirilli
Illustrator
Micah Piccirilli
Client
Michael Veinbergs

❶

Fine Handcrafts For Your Home

THE BUNGALOW INC.
6367 GUILFORD AVE., INDIANAPOLIS, IN 46220

D i a n e   S e y b e r t
J e n n i f e r   V e l a s c o
3 1 7 / 2 5 3 - 5 0 2 8

❷

D E B O R A H

H O F F M A N

writer

P.O. BOX 64883
TUCSON, AZ 85728

PHONE / FAX
602 ✦ 577 ✦ 2772

❸

Jeffrey Ross Music

High Tech Music

Jeffrey Ross
219 First Ave So., Suite 203
Seattle, WA 98104

206. 343. 5225

Marketing, Management,
Talent Development, Music Publishing

❹

O'LEARY
illustration
617·623·1989

❺

MICHAEL VEINBERGS
MAGICIAN

UCSD 9450
GILMAN DRIVE
BOX 926-830
LA JOLLA, CA 92092
619-558-8020
619-583-2450

❻

1

2

3

4

NEUBAUER
MAINTENANCE
8933 SOUTH 25TH STREET SCOTTS, MICHIGAN 49088
TEL (616) 327-7343
LANDSCAPING
LAWNSERVICE
SNOWPLOWING
JEFF NEUBAUER

5

1 Design Firm
CAW
Designer
Carsten-Andres Werner
Client
das niedrig-energie Haus GmbH
Architecture

2 Designer
Andreas Weiss
Client
Rosa Jaisli
Sculptor

3 Design Firm
Ampersand Design Group
Designer
Dan González
Client
Self-promotion
Graphic design

4 Design Firm
The Woldring Company
Designer
Robert Woldring
Client
Jeff Neubauer
Lawn services

5 Design Firm
Jeff Labbé Design 0950
Designer
Jeff Labbé
Client
Self-promotion
Design

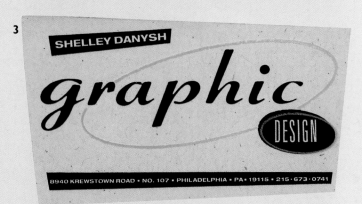

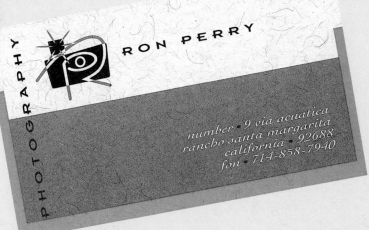

1 Design Firm
Jeff Labbé Design 0950
Designer
Jeff Labbé
Client
Conn Quigley
Shoe repair

2 Design Firm
V. Allen Crawford Design
Designer
V. Allen Crawford
Client
Victoria Sadowski
Independent metalsmith

3 Design Firm
Shelley Danysh Studio
Designer
Shelley Danysh
Client
Self-promotion
Graphic design

4 Design Firm
Giorgio Davanzo Design
Designer
Giorgio Davanzo
Client
Julie Cascioppo
Cabaret and jazz vocalist

5 Design Firm
Jeff Labbé Design 0950
Designer
Jeff Labbé
Client
Ron Perry
Photography

1

Betsy Crone

3107 Hawthorne Street, NW

Washington, DC 20008

Telephone 202-342-0997

Fax 202-342-0995

2

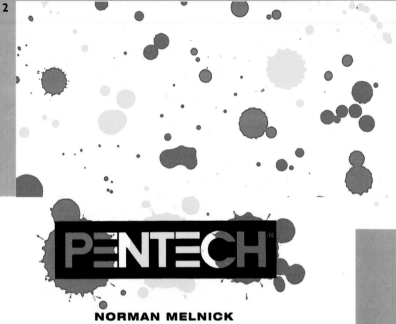

NORMAN MELNICK
CHAIRMAN

PENTECH INTERNATIONAL, INC.
DURHAM CENTER   2 ETHEL ROAD   EDISON   NJ   08817
908·287·6640 **FAX** 908·287·6610

3

Sara Gray
Electronic Publishing
415 854 7065

P.O. Box 7725
Menlo Park, CA 94026
Fax 415 854 5042
AppleLink: gray.pub

4

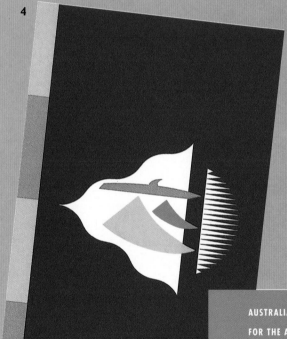

AUSTRALIAN CHALLENGE

FOR THE AMERICA'S CUP

A.C.N. 008 559 920

INCORPORATED IN A.C.T.

CHALLENGING THROUGH

AUSTRALIAN YACHT CLUB INC.

＊

EDMUNDS JONES PTY LTD

MARKETING MANAGEMENT

12/1-3 MANDOLONG ROAD

MOSMAN N.S.W. 2088

P.O. BOX 24

MILSONS POINT N.S.W. 2061

TELEPHONE (02) 960 3700

FACSIMILE (02) 960 3460

1 Design Firm
Market Sights, Inc.
Designer
Marilyn Worseldine
Client
Betsy Crone
Fund-raising consulting

2 Design Firm
Shelley Danysh Studio
Designer
Shelley Danysh
Client
Pentech International, Inc.
Writing instruments manufacturing

3 Design Firm
Stowe Designer
Designer
Jodie Stowe
Client
Sara Gray Electronic Publishing

4 Design Firm
Edmunds Jones Design
Designer
Cate Edmunds
Client
Sydney, Australia Americas Cup Boat
Sailboat

1

Sue McGarry
5404 McCoy
Shawnee Mission, KS 66226
913•441•0818 (home)
913•722•6505 x242

JuJu BEADS

2

C PICTURES

DONNA WOELFFER

2811 MCKINNEY NO. 204

DALLAS, TEXAS 75204

PHONE 214 855 0557

FAX 214 855 5068

3

46 Waltham Street Studio 307 Boston MA 02118
Phone: (617) 426-6479   Fax: (617) 426-5266

Susan Muldoon
Designer/Illustrator

1 Design Firm
Eat Design
Art Director
Patrice Eilts-Jobe
Designers
Patrice Eilts-Jobe, Kevin Tracy
Illustrator
Kevin Tracy
Client
JuJu Beads
Bead collector and jeweler

2 Design Firm
Peterson & Company
Designer
Bryan L. Peterson
Client
C-Pictures
Photographer's representative

3 Design Firm
M Design
Designer
Susan Muldoon
Client
Self-promotion
Design studio

4/5 Design Firm
One & One Design Consultants Inc.
Designer
Dominick Sarcia
Client
Tom Black
Professional woodworking

4

TOM BLACK

AUTHORIZED
FACTORY SERVICE
FOR DELTA MACHINERY

SERVICE ON OTHER
MAJOR BRANDS

13 DAPHNE COURT,
EDISON, N.J. 08820
1-908-668-1569

TOM BLACK

PROFESSIONAL
WOODWORKING.
PRODUCT
DEMONSTRATION.
SEMINARS AND
INSTRUCTION.

13 DAPHNE COURT,
EDISON, N.J. 08820
1-908-668-1569

Geek Squad
computer support services
212 Third Avenue North, Suite 579
Minneapolis, Minnesota 55401

Robert C. Stephens
geek-squad@bitstream.mpls.mn.us
tel. 612.751.6205
fax. 612.288.9983

1

Geek Squad

2

M

MIM'S BAKERY

let 'em
eat cake
let 'em
eat cake
let 'em
eat cake

890 HUMBOLDT AVE
CHICO, CA 95928
916 345 3331

3

ART SPACE

REGAN JACKSON

ART DIRECTION

TEL: 310.841.6061

FAX: 310.841.0350

4

REAL FAST DELIVERY!

QUALITY DOESN'T COST! *IT PAYS!*

CALL US TODAY!

WURTSBAUGH
SPECIALTY MARKETING SERVICES

731 Carman Meadows Drive
Manchester, Missouri 63021
☎ **(314) 227-5615** ☎

MARTHA WEGMANN, PRESIDENT

ALMOST ANY PLACE!

1

YOU CAN'T LOSE!

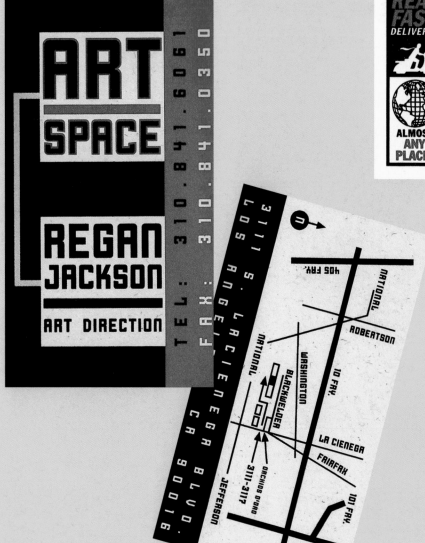

1 Design Firm
Stress Lab
Designer
Chuck Hermes
Client
Geek Squad
Computer support services

2 Design Firm
Wiedemann Design
Designer
Frank Wiedemann
Client
Mim's Bakery

3 Design Firm
13th Floor
Art Director
Regan Jackson
Designer
Eric Ruffing
Client
Regan Jackson
Art direction

4 Design Firm
Phoenix Creative
Designer
Eric Thoelke
Client
Wurtsbaugh
Specialty marketing services

eric ruffing

vox.310.546.7135
fax 310.546.6234

3309 pine av
manhattan beach
california
9 0 2 6 6

⑬

ourmindswanderwhereothersfeartogo

1 3 T H F L O O R

1 Design Firm
13th Floor
Art Directors
Dave Parmley, Eric Ruffing
Designers
Dave Parmley, Eric Ruffing
Illustrator
Dave Parmley
Client
Self-promotion
Graphic design

2 Design Firm
Choplogic
Designer
Walter McCord
Client
La Peche
Restaurant

3 Design Firm
Leslie Chan Design Co., Ltd.
Designer
Leslie Chan Wing Kei
Illustrator
Toto Tseng
Client
Giurlani Ristorante Italiano
Restaurant

4 Design Firm
PhD
Designer
Terri Haas
Client
Body & Soul
Swedish sport accupressure

5 Design Firm
Shields Design
Art Director
Charles Shields
Designer
Juan Vega
Illustrator
Juan Vega
Client
Tech Source
Macintosh sales and service

LA PÊCHE I
GOURMET TO GO & CATERING
1147 BARDSTOWN ROAD
LOUISVILLE, KY 40204
TEL: (502) 451·0377

Michelle Bartholomew

LA PÊCHE II
CAFE & GOURMET TO GO
HOLIDAY MANOR CENTER
4941 BROWNSBORO ROAD
LOUISVILLE, KY 40222
TEL: (502) 339·7593

Ruffino Ristorante Italiano
No. 15, Lane 25, Shuang Cheng St., Taipei, Taiwan
Tel : (02) 592-3355
Giurlani Ristorante Italiano
B2 No. 203, Tun Hwa S. Road Sec. 2, Taipei, Taiwan
Tel : (02) 377-0899, 377-0931

意庭意大利餐廳
總店・台北市雙城街25巷15號
電話：(02) 592-3355
遠企店・台北市敦化南路二段203號B 2
電話：(02) 377-0899, 377-0931

Giurlani
RISTORANTE ITALIANO

BODY & SOUL

swedish

sport

Mary Mitchell • Therapeutic Massage • 203.535.3039

acupressure

Nationally Certified • AMTA Member

5110 E. Clinton Way

Suite 204

Fresno, CA 93727

209 252-8008

fax 252-0664

TECHSOURCE
Macintosh Sales & Service

Tom Siechert

a Cat's Garden

1

a Cat's Garden

2

Red Rhinoceros

WILLIAM KOLBER
Vice President

1466 BROADWAY SUITE 808
NEW YORK NEW YORK 10036
· TELEPHONE (212) 764 5100
FAX (212) 764 5213 / 5231

3

JEWEL RUFFIN

131 Jasper Drive
Amherst, NY 14226
716·838·0553

CHAMELEON
DESIGN LIMITED

4

TWO BEARS DANCING   1920 ABRAMS PARKWAY
TRADING COMPANY   SUITE 367
                                        DALLAS, TEXAS
SUE SWIGART   75214
PRESIDENT   214 733 9884

5

1 Design Firm
Hixson Design
Designer
Gary Hixson
Illustrator
Public Domain Engraving
Client
A Cat's Garden
Gift retail

2 Design Firm
Patricia Spencer Advertising & Design
Designer
Patricia Spencer
Client
Red Rhinoceros
Men's sportswear design

3 Design Firm
Chameleon Design Ltd.
Designer
Jewel Ruffin
Client
Self-promotion
Graphic design

4 Design Firm
Joseph Rattan Design
Designer
Joseph Rattan
Illustrator
Greg Morgan
Client
Two Bears Dancing
Trading Company
Native American jewelry
manufacturing

5 Design Firm
Lead Dog Communications
Designer
Suzanne Jacquot
Illustrator
Cliff Jew
Client
Self-promotion
Design and communications

1

Mark J Laughlin

617 437 1356
617 437 1406 Fax

LAUGHLIN
Winkler

Marketing + Design

4 Clarendon Street

Boston Massachusetts

02116 6117

2

MaRiaS SamS

g·r·a·p·h·i·c d·e·s·i·g·n

3310 Thompson Street
Richmond, Va. 23222
(804) 321-4866

3

10284 ROYAL ANN AVENUE

SAN DIEGO

CALIFORNIA · 92126

TEL 619.578.8799

FAX 619.578.8799

**STEVEN
MORRIS
DESIGN**

5

Toni·Voss

COPYWRITER
CREATIVE THINKER

455 HUNTERS RIDGE
SALINE • MI 48176
TEL 313•944•0024
FAX 313•944•0190

4

Kolibri
CREATIV HAIRSTYLING

Andrea Neher
A-6774 Tschagguns 487, Tel. 0 55 56 / 39 20

1 Design Firm
Laughlin/Winkler Inc.
Designers
Mark Laughlin, Ellen Winkler
Client
Self-promotion
Graphic design and marketing

2 Design Firm
Maria Sams Graphic Design
Designer
Maria Sams
Client
Self-promotion
Graphic design

3 Design Firm
Steven Morris Design
Designer
Steven Morris
Client
Self-promotion
Graphic design

4 Design Firm
Grafik Design Ganahl Christoph
Designer
Ganahl Christoph
Client
Kolibri
Hair salon

5 Design Firm
elDesign
Art Director
Lynn St. Pierre
Designer
Lynn St. Pierre
Illustrator
Kevin Ewing
Client
Toni Voss
Copywriter

1

MERCEDES McDonald

ILLUSTRATOR

1939 ATHENDUR COURT
SAN JOSE CA 95120 408 268 0662

2

ARTEFACTO

diseño

RODOLFO
AREVALO

schiller114-3
polanco11570

5 3 1 0 3 5 7
9 0 5 4 1 3 6 2 5 2

3

KAĞAN ATSÜREN
TASARIM
İLLÜSTRASYON
0 - 212 273 18 01
YAŞARBEY SK
9/8 80310
MECIDIYEKÖY
İSTANBUL

4

Vision Landscape

J.G. Hayes

87 Dickson Avenue

Arlington, MA 02174

617.945.8936

Award Winning

Garden Design

5

Paisley Park Graphics

Lizz Luce·Graphic Artist
7801 Audubon Road
Chanhassen MN 55317
(612) 474 6620
(612) 474 4949 FAX

❶
Design Firm
Power Design
Designer
Pat Power
Client
Nancy Blaine

❷
Design Firm
Mark Palmer Design
Art Director
Mark Palmer
Designers
Mark Palmer, Pat Kellogg
Illustrators
Mark Palmer, Pat Kellogg
Client
Scribbler's Ink

❸
Design Firm
Rick Eiber Design
Art Director
Rick Eiber
Designer
Rick Eiber
Illustrator
Norman Hathaway
Client
Trade-Marx Sign &
Display Corp.

❹
Design Firm
Ascent Communications
Art Director
Allen Haeger
Designer
Allen Haeger
Client
American Design

❺
Design Firm
Kym Abrams Design
Art Director
Kym Abrams
Designer
Kym Abrams
Client
Julia Ryan Retouching

1 Design Firm
Karen Barranco Design & Illustration
Designer
Karen Barranco
Client
Etienne Bresson
Women's clothing design

2 Design Firm
Becker Design
Designer
Neil Becker
Client
Wave Property Management

3 Design Firm
Choplogic
Art Directors
Walter McCord, Mary Cawein
Designer
Walter McCord
Client
Langsford Center
Speech and reading specialists

4 Design Firm
Choplogic
Art Directors
Walter McCord, Mary Cawein
Designer
Walter McCord
Client
Bruce Carnahan
Landscape architecture

1

Etienne Bresson

• designer • stylist •

213 656 1229

2

Lance Lichter   W62 N551   414.375.6868 *p*
President   Washington Ave.   414.375.6869 *f*
   Cedarburg, WI
   53012

WAVE
Property Management
~

3

G. STEPHEN McCROCKLIN, DIRECTOR

THE LANGSFORD CENTER
LEARNING TO EXCEL

4

214 Albany Avenue
Louisville, Kentucky 40206
(—)6-1818

Bruce Carnahan Landscape Design

1

DONNA L. ROBINSON

Certified Public Accountant

TEL 404·423·9997
FAX 404·427·5819
1256 COBB PARKWAY N.
MARIETTA, GA 30062

CERTIFIED PUBLIC ACCOUNTANTS
PATRICK W LACEY
PC
DEDICATED TO EXCELLENCE

2

JOHN WAGNER

PHOTOGRAPHY

212 THIRD AVENUE NORTH SUITE 380
MINNEAPOLIS MINNESOTA 55401
TELEPHONE 612-330-0946 FAX 612-330-0035

3

GEORGIE MEL B. RACELA
Certified Public Accountant
CERTIFICATE NO. 88266

535 Gen. Luis Street
Novaliches
Quezon City

Telephone : 936-2440

4

unit 19,   ben briggs
                           director
21 cohen court,
clovelley park,
SA 5042,
australia
tel: 276 5914
fax: 2765915

R A J
THE CLOTHING COMPANY

5

900 Lay Road

St. Louis, MO 63124

Telephone

314-991-0005

Facsimile   Chris Green

314-991-1512

Community School

1 Design Firm
Wages Design
Designer
Rory Myers
Client
Patrick W. Lacey
Certified public accountant

2 Design Firm
Stress Lab
Designer
Lizz Luce
Client
John Wagner
Photography

3 Design Firm
Design Source, Inc.
Designer
Robert Salazar
Client
Georgie Racela
Certified public accountant

4 Design Firm
Isheo Design House
Designer
Ishmael Sheo
Client
RAJ - The Clothing Company
Boutique

5 Design Firm
Kiku Obata & Company
Art Director
Amy Knopf, Kiku Obata
Designer
Amy Knopf
Illustrator
Sara Love
Client
Community School
Private elementary school

6 Design Firm
Isheo Design House
Designer
Ishmael Sheo
Client
JAM - Street Wear
Clothing maufacturing

6

SAM LEE

Jam STREET WEAR

51, CECIL STREET,
HAMILTON,
WAIKATO AREA,
NEW ZEALAND
TEL: 8490113 FAX: 8492313

1

T R A C Y · S A B I N
G R A P H I C · D E S I G N
1 3 4 7 6 R I D L E Y R O A D
S A N D I E G O , C A 9 2 1 2 9
· P H O N E & F A X 6 1 9 . 4 8 4 . 8 7 1 2 ·

1 Design Firm
Tracy Sabin Graphic Design
Designer
Tracy Sabin
Client
Self-promotion
Design and illustration

2 Design Firm
Becker Design
Designer
Neil Becker
Client
Racine Danish Kringles
Bakery

3 Design Firm
THARP DID IT
Designer
Rick Tharp
Client
Artpath
*Public school volunteer
art programs*

4 Design Firm
Karen Barranco Design
& Illustration
Designer
Karen Barranco
Client
Sam Hurwitz Productions
Film production

5 Design Firm
Tangram Strategic Design
Art Director
Enrico Sempi
Designer
Enrico Sempi, Antonella Trevisan
Client
Schürch & Partners
Financial consulting

2

Michael D. Heyer
President

2529 Golf Avenue
Racine, Wisconsin 53404
Phone 414.633.1819
Toll Free 800.432.6474
Fax 414.774.4410

3

TRUDY ZIMMERMAN
Project Director

333 Art & Design Building
San Jose State University
San Jose, CA 95192-0089

FAX 408.924.4326
☎ 408.924.4360

A R T P A T H

4

TEL 213.871.6907

Sam Hurwitz Productions

11740 WILSHIRE BOULEVARD
SUITE A-1304
LOS ANGELES, CALIFORNIA 90025

FAX 310.473.9905

5

Schürch & Partners

H. Cäsar Schürch

Dufourstrasse 181, CH 8034 Zürich
Tel. 01 4224511, Fax 01 4227731

1

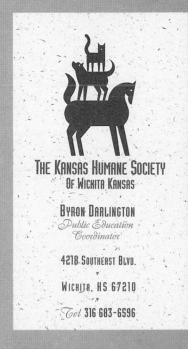

THE KANSAS HUMANE SOCIETY
OF WICHITA KANSAS

BYRON DARLINGTON
*Public Education
Coordinator*

4218 SOUTHEAST BLVD.

WICHITA, KS 67210

Tel 316 683-6596

2

D2 design

Dominique Duval
graphiste

6300, Avenue du Parc
Bureau 502
Montréal Québec
H2V 4H8

Téléphone
Télécopieur
(514) 495 1270

3

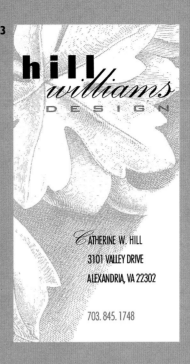

CATHERINE W. HILL

3101 VALLEY DRIVE

ALEXANDRIA, VA 22302

703. 845. 1748

4

ED PHELPS

desi2n

Two In Design

469 Oakdale Road

Suite A9

Atlanta, Georgia 30307

Telephone: [404] 523-6023

Fax: [404] 523-0311

5

GaryMyers

13111 WEST MARKHAM
SHADOW LAKE #274
LITTLE ROCK, AR 72211
501.221.2343

ILLUSTRATION
DESIGN

6

ITALIA
IN BOCCA

DELIKATESSEN

BARRA FREE SHOPPING
AV. DAS AMÉRICAS, 4.666
2° PISO - TEL. E FAX: 325 2963
2ª A SÁBADO DAS 10 ÀS 22H
DOMINGO DAS 14 ÀS 20H

1 Design Firm
Greteman Group
Designers
Sonia Greteman, Bill Gardner
Client
The Kansas Humane Society
Animal shelter

2 Design Firm
D2 Design
Designer
Dominique Duval
Client
Self-promotion
Graphic design

3 Design Firm
Barbara Raab Design
Art Director
Barbara Raab Sgouros
Designer
Lee Ann Rhodes
Client
Hill Williams Design
Interior decorating

4 Design Firm
Two In Design
Designer
Ed Phelps
Client
Two In Design
Graphic design

5 Design Firm
Gary Meyers
Designer
Gary Meyers
Client
Self-promotion
Illustration and design

6 Design Firm
Animus Comunicacáo
Art Director
Rique Nitzsche
Designer
Rique Nitzsche, Felício Torres
Illustrator
Antonino Homobono
Client
Italia in Bocca
Italian restaurant

1

2

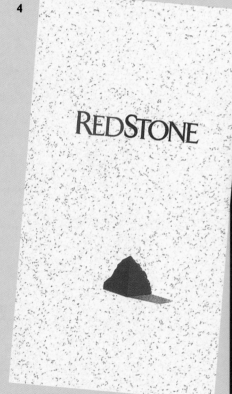

3

WA

WellerArchitects

Tel 5-05-255-8270

Fax 505-255-8830

401 Alvarado Drive SE

Suite D Albuquerque, New Mexico 87108

4

REDSTONE

RICH VLIET
President

DESIGN
DEVELOPMENT

144 N. MOSLEY

WICHITA, KS 67202

TEL 316 263 2711

FAX 316 263 4711

5

1 Design Firm
Peterson & Company
Art Directors
Dave Eliason, Bryan L. Peterson
Designer
Dave Eliason
Client
ACME Rubber Stamp Company

2 Design Firm
Vaughn Wedeen Creative
Designer
Rick Vaughn
Client
Rippelstein's
Men's clothing store

3 Design Firm
Vaughn Wedeen Creative
Designer
Rick Vaughn
Client
Weller Architects

4 Design Firm
Greteman Group
Art Directors
Sonia Greteman, James Strange
Designer
James Strange
Client
Red Stone
Design development

5 Design Firm
Greenbox Grafik
Designer
Christian Posch
Client
Self-promotion
Graphic design

1

DAVE SYFERD

☐ SUN VALLEY

207 Aspen Dr.
Ketcham, Idaho
83340
208 726 8837

☐ BOISE

350 N. 9th St.
P.O. Box 8283
Boise, Idaho
83707
208 342 0925

☐ SEATTLE

8006 Avalon Pl.
Mercer Island,
Washington
98040
206 232 3103

2

monica
GÖTZ
tofana

322 E 89 APT 4A
NEW YORK NY 10128
212 534 1559

3

associatie voor ontwerp ● advies

Proforma
[R DAM]

Joop Ridder
algemeen directeur

Slepersvest 5-7
3011 MK Rotterdam
(010) 411 27 22

associatie voor ontwerp ● advies

Proforma
[R DAM]

Els van Klinken
communicatieadviseur

Slepersvest 5-7
3011 MK Rotterdam

4

ARTEFAB

ALAIN LAUZON
Président
Directeur général

3820 E, rue Isabelle
Brossard, Québec
Canada, J4Y 2R3

Tél.: (514) 444 2224
Téléc.: (514) 444 2122

1 **Design Firm**
Hornall Anderson Design Works
Art Director
Jack Anderson
Designers
Jack Anderson, Heidi Favour,
Bruce Branson-Meyer
Client
Dave Syferd
Marketing and public relations

2 **Design Firm**
Monica Gîtz Design
Designer
Monica Gîtz
Client
Self-promotion
Graphic design

3 **Design Firm**
Proforma, Association of
Designers & Consultants
Art Director
Aad Van Dommelen
Client
Self-promotion
Design

4 **Design Firm**
D2 Design
Designer
Dominique Duval
Client
Artefab
*Opera and theatre
set construction*